WALKING IN YOUR

True Identity

SET FREE TO BE ALL
GOD DESIGNED YOU TO BE

STUDY GUIDE
GROUPS / INDIVIDUALS

JENNIFER BROMMET

WITH REMCO BROMMET, DEBBIE JONES & JUDY MILLS

978-0-9895626-8-3 - Paperback

Printed in the United States of America by Booklogix, Alpharetta, Georgia.

Cover design by Jennifer Brommet

Front Cover photo © Sawitree Pamee | Dreamstime.com
Back Cover photo © Cipariss | Dreamstime.com
Interior layout design by Jennifer Brommet
Editing by Carina Brommet
Judy Mills' Headshot by Emily Fletke Photography www.emilyfletkephotography.com

All Scripture quotations, unless otherwise indicated, are taken from The Holy Bible, *English Standard Version*, copyright © 2001 by Crossway Bibles, a division of Good news Publishers. Used by permission. All rights reserved.

All other scripture notations can be found on page 120.

Includes bibliographical references

This book may be purchased in bulk for educational, small group or church use.
For information please contact: Jennifer Brommet, www.TrueIdentityStudy.com or www.TrueIdentityMinistries.org.

Dedication

*For the glory and honor of Jesus Christ,
Who gives us all we need to walk freely
in all He designed us to be!*

Contents

Introduction

Congratulations! You have successfully completed the *True Identity Study* and have now arrived at your next destination: *Walking in Your True Identity*.

As we discussed in the *True Identity Study*, learning to walk and live in your true identity is not a quick fix, it's a process. Many of you who have done the *True Identity Study* have asked if we had something to follow it to help you continue in that process, and now we do with this new *Walking in Your True Identity Study*!

The *True Identity Study* introduced you to understanding your personality, identifying and renouncing lies, and replacing them with God's truths of who He has designed you to be. We focused primarily on the first part of your true identity: Who you are in Christ. Now we are going to take you a step further and explore the second part of your true identity: Who Christ is in you.

Our prayer is that this study will not only deepen your awareness and practical understanding of Jesus living in you through the Holy Spirit, but also help you get a clearer understanding of what God's design & purpose for your life is and how to walk in that design through: understanding your salvation, knowing intimacy with God, understanding & embracing your partnership with the Holy Spirit, and trusting God in taking steps of faith to walk consistently in your true identity.

We've changed things up a little bit with this new study. I've asked a few of my friends to collaborate with me in the development and writing of this study. The elements of each session are similar, but we've changed the order and format a bit.

A significant part of maturing in your faith walk with God is to learn how to study the Bible for yourself, hear from God, and in partnership with the Holy Spirit, put what you are learning and hearing into action. The format of this study is designed to help you do that.

His call to you through this study is: "Come closer!" We pray this study will indeed deepen your understanding and relationship with God, allowing you to walk in new levels of freedom in your true identity in Him.

As with the True Identity Study, open your heart to what the Lord desires to work out in you through this study as He continues to set you free from lies & strongholds and brings you into a place of deeper trust and joy in your faith walk with Him. We hope this study will bless you as much as it did for us in writing it.

Are you ready? Let's go for a walk!

Jennifer Brommet & Study Team

1

ACCESS TO SESSION VIDEOS & AUDIO

To access the video for each session, go to the web link below or scan the QR code below with your phone. All session videos and audio of videos are on a *Walking In Your True Identity Study* web page that is only accessible via these links. Videos are listed in order by session. The videos web page link is also on the Session Author Video page of each session. There is no extra fee to access the videos.

www.TrueIdentityStudy.com/walking-ti-videos-audio

**Session Videos
QR Code**

**Access videos & audio
through your phone**

How to Use This Study Guide

We're excited that you completed the first *True Identity Study* and now taking the next step in deepening your relationship with the Lord with this *Walking In Your True Identity Study!* As mentioned in the Introduction, this study is arranged a bit differently. There is an introduction video and then 7 main study sessions, with the session segments ordered differently (see below). The study was designed to help you engage in personal in-depth self-study and develop habits of abiding in Christ. The more you invest in this study the more you will experience the life changing power of walking in your true identity! (See *Self-Study Helps* on Page 5)

As before, this study can be used either individually or in a small group setting. If you are doing this study as a group, each person in the group should have his or her own Study Guide. **Each session includes:** relevant Scripture, in-depth self-study with Core Principles and reflection questions, group discussion questions, an activity to help apply what you have learned, smaller group prayer focus, and resources for further study.

INSTRUCTIONS FOR THE STUDY & GROUP

- Each session begins with Scripture and brief introduction to the session, *but instead of following along with a teaching video*, you will do the session **SELF-STUDY** with Core Principles *on your own*. This is followed by **REFLECTION QUESTIONS** that will help you dig a little deeper in each session. Pray before you begin and ask the Lord to teach you and speak to you as you do this self study portion. Allow yourself about 45 minutes to an hour to complete this first part.

- Then, **when you come together as a group**, you will go through the **GROUP DISCUSSION QUESTIONS**. Be sure to do the Self-Study and Reflection Questions *before* you meet with your group. If you have not completed these, then we encourage you to refrain from answering the Group Discussion Questions with your group.

- **After the Group Discussion Questions** you will watch a brief **VIDEO** by the author of that session, with a session overview and personal example. **Access each session video or audio file with the web link or QR Code on Page 2.**

- **After the video**, you'll have as in the previous study, **WALKING IT HOME - APPLYING WHAT YOU HAVE LEARNED**, with a smaller group activity to begin putting into practice what you're learning, then **PRAYING IT FORWARD**, with time to pray together. This is followed by session **RESOURCES** for additional study/information.

- Remember that everything shared in the group is confidential and not to be shared outside the group. This will help build a loving, trusting, and safe environment to heal, be set free and grow together. Sharing personal examples or information is always optional. Keep in mind that when you share, your testimony may encourage or help someone else.

- Refrain from discussing church, politics, books, movies or anything that would have the potential to divide the group. Eliminate distractions and keep your cell phones off.

INSTRUCTIONS FOR GROUP LEADERS

A group leader will be needed for each session. You may want to select one person, or you can share the responsibility.

- As a leader you will continue to set the stage for a loving and accepting environment where everyone can feel comfortable sharing and going deep with God together.

- You will bring a sense of belonging and unity to the group, facilitate discussions and refrain from teaching, preaching or counseling. The key in this study is to encourage participants to invest in the self-study and grow in their understanding of the Bible.

- At the beginning of the study, review the new order of the sessions for this study.

- Explain the use of the facility and location of restrooms if meeting in-person. If meeting Online, review Online guidelines and etiquette, including keeping cell phones off.

- 90 minutes are allowed for each session; the facilitator keeps the focus on the study and on time. **You will start each session with the Group Discussion Questions** and will have more time for discussion and activities since the teaching portion of the study is done through self-study individually before each group meets. *Remind everyone to complete the Self-Study and Reflection Questions BEFORE you meet each week.*

- If participants have *not* done the Self-Study and Reflection Questions, encourage them to refrain from answering Group Discussion Questions. You may have to give a brief overview of the session topic to bring everyone up to speed. Keep encouraging them to do the self-study and reflection questions for their own personal growth and ability to engage in group discussion.

- Open and close each session with a brief prayer.

- Be prepared to show the session VIDEO *after* the Group Discussion Questions in each session.

- As in the previous study, encourage the group to go to God in listening prayer throughout the study. There is also a session in this study focused on this topic.

Note to Group Leader
Prepare for each session by doing your own Self-Study, Reflection Questions, and getting familiar with the Discussion Questions. Also review the session to see if there are recommended special activities or materials needed for an activity.

See *Additional Resources for Group Leaders* on Page 117 for more details on leading a group.

Suggestions for an Introduction Session and/or Closing Ceremony
(Optional, and can be done as an additional group meeting)

- **As you start this study** - Take time to recap the *True Identity Study* highlights, and how God has been working in the lives of participants since finishing that study. Review the new sessions set-up and order for this study.

- **After completing this study** - Large group sharing time - allow for participants to share how God spoke to them or what He revealed to them in this current study.

- Communion and Fellowship meal ending with prayer for one another.

May you be blessed as you facilitate and shepherd your group through this transformational study!

Self-Study Helps

As mentioned above, this *Walking In Your True Identity* study is set up a bit differently from the first *True Identity* study. A key to growth in your faith walk and maturity in your relationship with God is to learn to study the Bible for *yourself*. God wants to bring us into intimacy with Himself. Therefore, it is not just *reading* Scripture or going off what someone else has said about it, but discovering there is nothing more exciting than learning how to dig deeper into God's Word and allowing *Him* to etch His truth on your heart, mind and life, transforming you from the inside out!

You may be new to this type of study and feel a bit overwhelmed, but as Kay Arthur says, *"The Bible was written so that anyone who wants to know who God is and how they are to live in a way that pleases Him can read it and find out."* Stick with this, and step by step it will become easier and a more natural way of study for you. Invest in this type of study and you will reap many rewards! Below are some self-study helps and resources to help you get started.

HELPS FOR SELF-STUDY

- **Gather Materials** - Have your *Walking In Your True Identity Study Guide*, Bible, pen, highlighter, and also phone or computer if you'd like to look up verses and resources Online as you study. Some also like to have a journal for keeping personal prayers and notes in.

- **Pray** - As you begin your study time, ask the Lord to lead you, give you understanding, and speak to you personally as you are looking up Bible verses, working through the Core Principles, and answering questions.

- **Look up Bible Verses** - Take the time to look up the Bible verses listed *throughout* the study. This will help you become more familiar with where these Scripture verses are in your Bible, as well as you can underline, highlight or make notes in your Bible for future reference. (See information about Bible translations on Page 8)

- **Dig Deeper** - Look up Scripture Online in various translations, check out the original Greek or Hebrew meaning of some of the words, and/or cross reference the Scripture verse with other Scripture. Ask the W's & H (who, what, when, where, why & how) questions. Get a full picture of the background and context of the Scripture. (**John 8:32**)

- **Ask God** - If you come across something you do not understand, stop and pray and ask the Lord to give you His understanding and wisdom (**James 1:5**). Also ask Him to reveal any insight or truth He wants you to know about what you are studying.

- **Take Notes** - As you work your way through the Self-Study, Core Principles and Reflection Questions, write down anything that stands out to you, speaks to you, or the Lord reveals to you. Also write down any questions you have that you may wish to do more study on later or ask another mature believer to help you with.

- **Application** - This study is not just to increase your knowledge *about* God and the Bible, but for you to allow the Lord to work *in you* and answer the question, *"How does what I am learning apply to me and my life?",* put into action the principles and biblical truths you are learning and make them an everyday reality of your faith walk! Remember, as a saved child of God, you have the Holy Spirit living in you to help you. (**Proverbs 23:12**)

- **Praise God** - Thank God for all He is doing in your life throughout this study! He loves you dearly, wants to deepen His relationship with you and continue to set you free from anything keeping you from living out the purpose and plans He has for your life! (**Isaiah 25:1; Jeremiah 29:11**)

SELF-STUDY RESOURCES
There are many books and Online resources available to help you with Bible self-study. Here are a few we recommend:

Study Bible - there are many Study Bibles in various translations. They often include study notes, maps and illustrations, charts, timelines, insightful explanations, teaching, and reference material.

Bible Dictionary - look up definitions of biblical words. Available in book form or Online.

Bible Concordance - many Bibles have a concordance in the back listing words with Scripture references using that word. You can also purchase a Bible Concordance or look one up Online. One recommended is the *The New Strong's Expanded Exhaustive Concordance of the Bible.*

Bible Commentaries - Bible commentaries aid in the study of Scripture by providing explanation and interpretation of Biblical text. We recommend you use commentaries *after* you have first done in-depth Bible study on your own, so that you do not become dependent on what others are saying or how they are interpreting Scripture instead of studying on your own first. Commentaries can be helpful for further insight and explanation when needed.

The New How to Study Your Bible - Discover the Life-Changing Approach to God's Word - *by Kay & David Arthur and Pete De Lacy.* This book fleshes out the inductive Bible study method with the 3 main key principles for Bible study - Observation, Interpretation and Application.

Online Resources
Some of the books mentioned above are also available Online. The Online resources for Bible study helps are limitless, but here are some we recommend:
(NOTE: Many of these listed also have an App to access information from your phone.)

Bible Gateway - https://www.biblegateway.com/
Bible Hub - https://biblehub.com/
Bible.Org - https://bible.org/
Blue Letter Bible - https://www.blueletterbible.org/
YouVersion - https://www.youversion.com/ or The Bible App

SOAP study method - https://lovegodgreatly.com/how-to-soap/
Lectio-Divina method - lectio-divina https://bustedhalo.com/ministry-resources/lectio-divina-beginners-guide
(See *Resources in Session 5 - Intimacy with God* on Page 47 for more detail on these methods.)

THREE PRINCIPLES FOR STUDYING THE BIBLE

How to Study the Bible *by Watchman Nee*; 1993, Living Stream Ministry.

1. A person must be reborn and filled with Holy Spirit. The Bible was inspired by Holy Spirit and written by men. It is understood spirit to spirit. (**1 Corinthians 2:14-16**)

2. A person must be walking according to Holy Spirit. If you are born again but still walking by the flesh in the ways of the world you will not have understanding when you read the Bible. Scripture says a man cannot serve two masters (**Matthew 6:24**). We have to choose whom we will serve as Joshua instructed the Israelites (**Joshua 24:15**), and then serve Him out of an obedient heart of love for Him.

3. Practice! **Hebrews 5:15** says –*"But solid food is for the mature, for those who have their powers of discernment trained by constant practice to distinguish good from evil."*

   And **Proverbs 25:2** says –*"It is the glory of God to conceal things, but the glory of kings is to search things out."*

We must be sincerely devoted to reading, meditating on and applying the Word of God. Remember, the author of the Bible is always present with you when you do.

ABOUT BIBLE TRANSLATIONS

You will notice that several different Bible translations are being used in this study. But what exactly is a Bible translation and why are there so many different ones?

The 66 books of the Bible were originally written in three different languages: The Old Testament in Hebrew and Aramaic, and the New Testament in Greek. For centuries, the only translation that existed was in Latin, the official language of the Roman Catholic Church, until John Wycliffe produced the first complete English translation in 1382. Since then, around 900 different English translations have been published.

It is important to know that translation from languages that are no longer used (Hebrew and Greek still exist but in quite different form than what was spoken in Bible times) always involves some interpretation. Even the chapters, verses, headings, and punctuation marks did not exist in the original texts!

A problem that translators face is that English does not always have an exactly equivalent word or grammatical term for what is written in the original language. Other dilemmas for translators is whether to emphasize the accurate form of words and sentences or their meaning, and how to make the translation relevant to our modern day use of language, which is constantly changing. For that reason, **four kinds of translation have emerged:**

1. **Formal equivalence** - a word-for-word rendering of each word and sentence from the original texts into their English equivalent. Examples of these are the King James Version, the New American Standard Bible and the English Standard Version.
2. **Functional equivalence** - rendering the thought behind the original text in English. An example of this is the New Living Translation. We're now inching away from translating literally and toward interpreting.
3. **Essential equivalence** - prioritize the essential meaning of a text over the literal form of the words. An example of essential equivalence is The Passion Translation.
4. **Paraphrase** – This is as far from word-for-word translation as you can go. A paraphrase takes a passage of Scripture and rewords it completely in everyday prose. The most famous example of this is The Message Bible.

Which translation to use is a matter of personal choice. In-depth studies benefit the most from formal equivalence translation, whereas devotional reading may benefit more from functional equivalence or essential equivalence, or even paraphrase. Those tend to be easier to read as well.

The writers of this study quote from nine different translations.
The one that is used most consistently and therefore unmarked is the ENGLISH STANDARD VERSION (ESV), which is the most recent formal equivalence translation of the original texts.

The other translations, noted each time in parentheses, are:

AMP - Amplified Bible (Regular and Classical Edition)   NLT - New Living Translation
NASB - New American Standard Bible   TLB - The Living Bible
NIV -   New International Version   TPT - The Passion Translation
NKJV - New King James Version

Session 1

Saved From

DEBBIE JONES

"For the wages of sin is death, but the free gift of God is eternal life in Christ Jesus our Lord."
Romans 6:23

"And the LORD God commanded the man, saying, "You may surely eat of every tree of the garden, but of the tree of the knowledge of good and evil you shall not eat, for in the day that you eat of it you shall surely die."
Genesis 2:16-17

"For all have sinned and fall short of the glory of God."
Romans 3:23

Understanding and walking in our true identity begins by understanding our salvation: what we have been saved from, how God saved us, and what we have been saved for. Our salvation is the foundation upon which our true identity in Christ is built. According to Ephesians 2:8 it is a gift from God, entered into by faith, and impossible to achieve by our own doing. Salvation from sin and death opens the way for restoration of our relationship with God. In this restored relationship He returns us to knowing and walking in our true identity and sets us free to be who He has designed us to be!

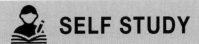

SELF STUDY

NOTE: Be sure to complete the Self Study, Core Principles, and Reflection Questions BEFORE you meet with your group each session.

Let's take a closer look at what God has saved us from – eternal death because of our sin. The lies we identified, renounced and replaced in the True Identity Study generally entered our souls through wounds, trauma and sin – our own and that of others. Remember, Satan wants to steal our true identity and keep us in bondage to lies and a "mistaken identity" for eternity.

Former Minnesota Viking turned evangelist Jeff Siemon said: *"The appreciation of one's salvation is only as great as the perception of one's peril."* In other words: to truly enjoy and live in wonder of our freedom in Christ, we must understand the eternal death He saved us from. Adam and Eve lived the perfect life in the Garden of Eden, but they chose to go their own way and eat from the tree of the knowledge of good and evil. When they did, life changed dramatically. They experienced shame and hid from God. They tried to cover their nakedness with fig leaves. They and the land were cursed. They were expelled from their home. They were separated from the very One who had created them and loved them. They experienced death. And it did not end there; every generation since has been born with a sin nature; every generation has experienced the curses that God inflicted on Adam and Eve. Mankind has been separated from the Creator by sin. Life has never been the same for anyone.

Continue your self study with the Core Principles below. Pray and ask the Lord to reveal any new insights, understanding or personal application. Look up all Scripture verses to become more familiar with where they are in your Bible, and make notes.

⚷ CORE PRINCIPLES

1. Sin Separates Us From God

Once expelled from Eden, Adam and Eve no longer walked with God in the cool of the day. Their intimacy with Him was different. If they wanted His presence, they had to seek Him, call upon Him, pray and hope to find Him – it required effort! Beginning with Adam and Eve, people were afraid of God and like Adam and Eve, hid from God.

2. The Result of Sin is Death

When Adam and Eve sinned, spiritual death came immediately; physical death came later. God created mankind in His image and likeness, but after the fall Genesis 5:3 says that Adam fathered a son in his own likeness, after his image. God is spirit; when Adam and Eve sinned, their spirit experienced death and so their offspring were born in the image and likeness of man. That is why Jesus told Nicodemus that he had to be born again, born of water and the Spirit to enter the Kingdom of God. Death is not confined to this world; it is also eternal, unless we are born again.

What exactly is spiritual, eternal death? The Bible is very explicit in telling us that those who do not turn to Christ will continue to live separated from God in a very unpleasant place called hell (Gehenna in Hebrew, or Hades in Greek).

Look up the following biblical descriptions and make note of anything the Lord reveals to you.

Revelation 20:15 - *"And if anyone's name was not found written in the book of life, he was thrown into the lake of fire."*

Matthew 8:12 - *"While the sons of the kingdom will be thrown into outer darkness. In that place there will be weeping and gnashing of teeth."*

Matthew 13:49b-50 - *"The angels will come and separate the evil from the righteous and throw them into the fiery furnace. In that place there will be weeping and gnashing of teeth."*

The prospect of eternal separation from God and spending eternity in a place of unimaginable anguish and punishment for not turning to Christ and continuing in sin should be enough for anyone to embrace salvation offered to us by a loving God. Every single member of the human race needs salvation and may receive it in faith.

 Every Generation Since Adam and Eve is Born with a Sin Nature

Have you ever noticed that you don't have to teach a young child to do what is evil, but you do have to teach them to do what is good?

Romans 3:23 tells us that all have sinned.

Romans 7:17-20 speaks of the presence and effect of the sin that dwells within.

2 Corinthians 5:17 refers to the new creation and the old which passes away when we are in Christ.

Without redemption through Jesus Christ, we cannot escape our sin nature.

4. There is No Hope for the Redemption of Mankind Apart from God

We cannot save ourselves no matter how good we think we are. There is only One who has the power to redeem us from death and that is Jesus Christ. He was God's plan from the beginning, before the foundation of the world.

However, mankind has been striving to get to heaven on his own since the Fall (see the story of the Tower of Babel in **Genesis 11**). Throughout Scripture, there are numerous examples of people going their own way instead of seeking and following God. Much of the history of Israel in the Old Testament is a tale of God's people rebelling against Him and going their own way despite prophetic warnings.

In the New Testament we have the example of Peter following his own ideas of discipleship rather than obeying Christ. They all amount to the same thing: We are not able to do anything to restore ourselves to God's plan. We are totally dependent on Him for redemption. Jesus said, *"I am the way, the truth, and the life. No one comes to the Father except through me."* (**John 14:6**)

5. God's Desire is to Redeem Mankind from the Fall and Restore His Creation to Perfection

God's heart is revealed in **Ezekiel 37:27**: *"My dwelling place shall be with them, and I will be their God, and they shall be my people."* He wants to live with us, He wants relationship with His people, and He wants His people to know Him as their God.

Jeremiah 29:11-15 is a familiar passage which also show us His desires for us –
"For I know the plans I have for you, declares the LORD, plans for welfare and not for evil, to give you a future and a hope. Then you will call upon me and come and pray to me, and I will hear you. You will seek me and find me, when you seek me with all your heart. I will be found by you, declares the LORD, and I will restore your fortunes and gather you from all the nations and all the places where I have driven you, declares the LORD, and I will bring you back to the place from which I sent you into exile."

God has not left us in an unredeemed state. He had a plan from the very beginning and that plan was Jesus. God knew that mankind would go its own way and yet He created us anyway. God has an answer, God *is* the answer. Jesus is the way, the truth and the life, and *no one* comes to the Father except through Him. The life we are saved from is desolate and barren because it is a life apart from the author of life; death is its ruler, and the people live in fear.

In our next session, we will take a closer look at how God saved us through Jesus, and what He saved us *for*.

✝ REFLECTION QUESTIONS

1. Read **Genesis 1-3** and **5:1-2**. Look carefully at what Adam and Eve had before they disobeyed God and sin entered into their life, and what they lost as a result of their disobedience. Enter your findings in the chart below.

What Adam and Eve had	What Adam and Eve lost
Example: Dominion over the earth	Their position of authority

2. Man was created on the 6th day, on the 7th day God rested from all He had done. This day of rest was man's first day. What do you think this implies? How do you think this changed after the fall of man?

3. Look at the curses listed in **Genesis 3:16-19**. How have you seen these curses operating in your life or in the lives of others?

4. "Slavery" is mentioned frequently in Scripture as a spiritual condition that controls us. Another word for it is "bondage." Look at **Galatians 5:1**, for example, where a "yoke of slavery" is mentioned. What that yoke consists of is further explained in **Galatians 4:1-7** and **Romans 7**. According to these passages what kind of life are believers saved from?

5. The lies we live with are a form of bondage – a yoke of slavery. We live our lives as slaves to what we believe when it is not in agreement with God's word. Have you been set free from a yoke of slavery? Describe what God set you free from when He delivered you from the lie to His truth.

6. We are told in **Luke 16:19-31** about the fate of a rich man and a beggar after death. What do you understand about this passage in light of what you have learned in this session about sin, the consequences of sin and eternal death?

Prayer:
"Father in heaven, thank you that you are both loving and righteous. Thank you that you chose to provide us with a way out of our sinfulness and out of eternal separation from you. Today I reaffirm my faith in Jesus Christ as my Savior and pray that you open my eyes to the significance of what I have been saved from so that I may reach a deeper enjoyment of my true identity in Christ and live in eternal gratitude of your mercy towards me. In Jesus' Name~ Amen."

👥 GROUP DISCUSSION QUESTIONS

1. What stood out to you in this session regarding:

    - sin

    - its power over people

    - its relationship to lies

    - its consequences for our relationship with God

2. In **Genesis 4:7**, God told Cain that he had to rule over sin. In **Romans 7:18**, the speaker says that he has the desire to do what is right but not the ability to carry it out.

    Why do you think God tells Cain to do something that he probably cannot do?

    What do you think God's message is to us?

3. Share what you listed in question one of Reflection Questions - what Adam and Eve had and what they lost as a result of their sin. How do you see these losses impacting humanity today?

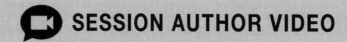

SESSION AUTHOR VIDEO

Watch the SESSION 1 - *SAVED FROM* author video

TrueIdentityStudy.com/walking-ti-videos-audio

DEBBIE JONES

Debbie gives an overview of Session 1 - *Saved From,* along with a personal example.

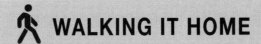

WALKING IT HOME

Divide into groups of two or three.

APPLYING WHAT YOU HAVE LEARNED

Discuss an experience you had that illustrates suffering consequences for sin, followed by forgiveness and restoration.

 **PRAYING IT FORWARD**

End the session by praying **Ephesians 3:14-19** over one another, and ask God to deepen our wonder for the depth of his love:

"For this reason I bow my knees before the Father, from whom every family in heaven and on earth is named, that according to the riches of His glory He may grant you to be strengthened with power through His Spirit in your inner being, so that Christ may dwell in your hearts through faith – that you, being rooted and grounded in love, may have strength to comprehend with all the saints what is the breadth and length and height and depth, and to know the love of Christ that surpasses knowledge, that you may be filled with all the fullness of God."

_____

_____

_____

_____

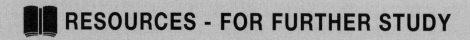
RESOURCES - FOR FURTHER STUDY

RECOMMENDED BOOKS:
Passion for Jesus - *by Mike Bickle*
Creation and The Fall - *by Gene Edwards*
The Utter Relief of Holiness and Moving Mountains - *by John Eldredge*
There were Two Trees in the Garden - *by Rick Joyner*
The Book of Mysteries – *by Jonathan Cahn*

NOTES

Session 2

Saved For

REMCO BROMMET

"Rejoice in the Lord always; again I will say, rejoice."
Philippians 4:4

Now that we have a better understanding of what we were saved from - sin and eternal separation from God (death) – we can delve into another important aspect of the foundation of our relationship with God: what we are saved *for*.

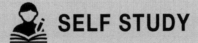

SELF STUDY

NOTE: Be sure to complete the Self Study, Core Principles, and Reflection Questions BEFORE you meet with your group each session.

Our salvation is God's response to repentance, which the New Testament shows to be a deep awareness and conviction of sin leading to a radical 180 degree turn toward a glad surrender to Jesus Christ as Savior, Lord, and Friend. For some that is a sudden, deeply emotional and radical experience akin to that of the major revivals of the 1700 and 1800's, but for many it is mostly a step of faith that forms the beginning of a gradual, but major life change.

The most important thing to remember is that as a result of our repentance we are forgiven (**Ephesians 1:7**), reconciled to God (**2 Corinthians 5:18**), adopted into His household as sons and daughters of God (our true identity!) (**Ephesians 1:5**), and filled with the Holy Spirit (**Ephesians 1:13**), who teaches us the mind of God (**John 14:26**), and changes us into the image of Christ from the inside out (**Romans 8:29**).

Acts 3:19-21 sums it all up in one text:

"Repent therefore, and turn again, that your sins may be blotted out, that times of refreshing may come from the presence of the Lord, and that he may send the Christ appointed to you, Jesus, whom heaven must receive until the time for restoring all the things about which God spoke by the mouths of his holy prophets long ago."

In short:
Conviction + Repentance + Surrender = Forgiveness + Salvation + Adoption + Rebirth + Delight in God

The release from the burden of our sinfulness that offended God and the fear of hell as punishment for our sin should lead to utter delight in the Savior and the desire to walk closely with Him from here to eternity.

What if I feel blah about my salvation or a daily relationship with God beyond asking Him to help me with my troubles? Perhaps then I have not fully understood what I have been saved from or saved for!

Continue your self study with the Core Principles below. Pray and ask the Lord to reveal any new insights, understanding or personal application. Look up all Scripture verses to become more familiar with where they are in your Bible, and make notes.

CORE PRINCIPLES

1. How God Saved Us

Now that we have established the transaction that restores our relationship with God (our repentance and surrender leading to forgiveness, spiritual rebirth, and a restored relationship with God) let's take a look at what God did to save us. He saved us by becoming one of us in the person of Jesus Christ, and in the form of a sinless human being subjecting himself to unimaginable torture and death, so that by His sacrifice the penalty for sin (condemnation to eternal punishment) would be paid once for all and we could be forgiven, redeemed, reconciled to Him, and adopted into His family as sons, daughters and co-heirs. We call that the atonement. His blood washed away our guilt, our need for punishment, our debt with God, as well as the power sin has over us.

The success of His atonement on the cross was proven by His resurrection. He was indeed the first human being to be raised from death into eternal life, with the promise that this would happen to anyone who places their faith in Him as Savior and Lord.

This salvation is not automatic. It becomes ours by repentance of our sin, placing our faith in Christ as our Savior and surrender to Him as Lord. Let these verses speak for themselves:

John 3:16 - *"For God so loved the world that he gave his only Son, that whoever believes in him should not perish but have eternal life."*

Romans 5:8 - *"But God shows his love for us in that while we were sinners, Christ died for us."*

Philippians 2:6-8 - *"…who, though he was in the form of God, did not count equality with God a thing to be grasped, but emptied himself by taking the form of a servant, being born in the likeness of men. And being found in human form, he humbled himself by becoming obedient to the point of death, even death on a cross."*

1 John 4:9-10 - *"In this the love of God was made manifest among us, that God sent his only Son into the world, so that we might live through him. In this is love, not that we have loved God, but that he loved us and sent his Son to be the propitiation for our sins."*

It should stir us deeply that God so loved the people who He created and who rebelled against Him wanting to be their own god, that He lowered Himself to become a human being in the person of Jesus Christ, revealed the principles of His kingdom, and then voluntarily subjected Himself to rejection, humiliation and the most horrible execution ever invented by a human society so He could take the penalty we deserve upon Himself. His blood paved the way for our reconciliation to Him, our access to Him and our relationship to Him as our Father, our right to call ourselves His children, and our enjoyment of His Presence in our daily life. Not to mention His provision, His protection, His promises, His comfort, His wisdom – all His blessings!

We Are Saved to Enjoy Him

Dr. John Piper has stated in his book *Desiring God* that the statement from the Westminster Catechism *"The chief end of man is to glorify God **and** enjoy Him forever"* should actually read *"The chief end of man is to glorify God **by** enjoying Him forever."* We fall short of that chief end because of sin and its urge to glorify ourselves. It is restored when we are brought back into relationship with God.

Dr. Piper has restated that chief end of man as follows: *"God is most glorified in us, when we are most satisfied in Him."*

Our highest form of worship, of glorifying God, is by saying: *"Nothing gives me greater delight, greater joy, greater satisfaction than knowing you and being in your Presence!"*

Knowing our true identity – who we are in Christ and who Christ is in us, begins by knowing what we were saved *for*. It helps us detach ourselves from the mistaken identity and the pleasures that our three-dimensional material world tries to give us, and attach ourselves to God, how He sees us and the pleasures that are found in His company. This is both a crucial, and beautiful, aspect of God's design for our lives as His sons and daughters.

1 Peter 2:11 says: *"Beloved, I urge you as sojourners and exiles to abstain from the passions of the flesh, which wage war against your soul."*

Sojourners and exiles just pass through and have no emotional attachment to their environment. Their attachment is to their destination. In our case, that is heaven, where God is. Emotional attachment to the world keeps sucking us back into our mistaken identity. Emotional attachment to God keeps us growing closer to Him and prepares us for an eternity in His presence.

Dr. John Piper, once more: *"Christ did not die to forgive sinners who go on treasuring anything above seeing and savoring God. And people who would be happy in heaven if Christ were not there, will not be there. The gospel is not a way to get people to heaven; it is a way to get people to God. It's a way of overcoming every obstacle to everlasting joy in God. If we don't want God above all things, we have not been converted by the gospel."*

A core part of our true identity is that we treasure Christ above all other things. The more we are set free from the lies that make up our mistaken identity and replace them with biblical truths of who we are in Him and Who He is in us, the deeper our love grows for Him and the more we treasure Him. And to treasure Him is to enjoy Him.
But how do we do that?

How to Enjoy God

If this study catches you feeling blah about your salvation and your relationship with the invisible God, or wondering how to delight in God in a world that is so full of turmoil, take heart. You are not alone. The Scriptures are filled with such struggles. And God knows, understands, and helps those who are honest with Him. Here are some steps that I have found useful:

1. **Enjoying God as your Father and Friend begins by seeking Him** – not for what He can do for you, but for Who He is. Make these your daily prayers, straight from how the Bible teaches us to pray for ourselves:

   Psalm 119:36 - *"Incline my heart to your testimonies and not to selfish gain."*

   Psalm 86:11 - *"O Lord I will walk in Your truth. Unite my heart to fear (=revere) your Name."*

   Psalm 90:14 - *"Satisfy us in the morning with Your steadfast love, that we may rejoice and be glad all our days."*

2. **Enjoying God grows through worship** – meditating on His goodness and glory. It takes your eyes off the pleasures of the world, directs them to God, and opens them to His glory. The Psalms are full of descriptive language of His glory to help you.

   While it is good to give thanks in all things, acknowledging that all things come from God, it is even better to worship and adore Him. Thanksgiving focuses on what He does, worship on Who He is!

3. **Enjoying God requires intentionally slowing down.** John Mark Comer has stated in his book *The Ruthless Elimination of Hurry* that he believes the main problem for Christians is not unbelief but busyness. Crowded schedules, fast-paced living, non-stop interaction with our electronic devices all conspire to program our minds and hearts away from God. We are literally losing our ability to meditate on spiritual truths and communicate with God in our spirits. Not to mention the fact that when we constantly nibble at the table of the world, we lose our appetite for God's menu.

Here are four practical suggestions for everyday life.
Make some notes of how you can begin implementing them:

- *Protect your Sabbath day.* Use it as a day of rest and prayer as it was intended, not to catch up with chores. Let your soul catch up with your body. It doesn't have to be Sunday. Just build a period of rest into your week. If you have a busy family that constantly demands your time and attention, you may need to get creative. Above all, try to train them in taking a Sabbath with you by doing fun and restful things together.

- *Slow down your daily pace*, from the speed with which you drive to how fast you walk. It will de-escalate the stress chemicals in your body and increase your sense of peace.

- *Limit interaction with your smartphone.* Its constant use wrecks our attention span.

- *Be in the moment:* look around you, smell the roses, and seek God, rather than letting your mind wander or worry about the next item on your to-do list.

The Bottom Line
God desires the pleasure of your company! He wants to reveal Himself to you, for your joy, and derives great pleasure out of knowing that you treasure and enjoy Him above all else in the universe. That is a reality worth embracing and growing into!

✝ REFLECTION QUESTIONS

1. Meditate on this invitation from God to you in **Isaiah 55:1-3:**

    "Come, everyone who thirsts, come to the waters; and he who has no money, come, buy and eat! Come, buy wine and milk without money and without price. Why do you spend your money for that which is not bread, and your labor for that which does not satisfy? Listen diligently to me, and eat what is good, and delight yourselves in rich food. Incline your ear and come to me; hear, that your soul may live; and I will make with you an everlasting covenant, my steadfast, sure love for David."

    These are God's thoughts about us being busy wasting time and money on things that don't last or satisfy, all the while missing out on what He has to offer: Endless delight and the richest of fares in Him. You just have to learn to see it!

    * Ask God to open your eyes to the richest of fares He has for you in Christ

    * Say *"Yes!"* to His invitation to partake

    * Praise Him for His unspeakable love in giving His life voluntarily to save you from eternal hell and unto an eternal relationship of joy in Him.

2. Spend time journaling through things in your daily life you must eliminate to focus more on God. You could list them and write out how you plan to reorder your life.

3. Take a journey down these Scriptures that express and describe joy in God.
   Look up each verse, and write down any thoughts, feelings or insights.

Nehemiah 8:10

Psalm 16:11

Isaiah 61:10

Habakkuk 3:17-19

John 15:11

Acts 2:28

Romans 14:17

Romans 15:13

Philippians 4:4-7

Rev. 7:15-17

Rev. 19:6-7

Prayer
"Dear heavenly Father, I confess that I am often distracted by the pleasures and comforts of this world and struggle to enjoy you above all else. Today I pray that you incline my heart to find my deepest joy in you. Please help me to slow down and get to know your presence by living in the moment. Grant me wisdom on how to reorder my life to remove distractions and deepen my awareness of your Presence. In Jesus' Name ~ Amen."

👥 GROUP DISCUSSION QUESTIONS

1. What have you learned about the importance of your salvation? How has that impacted your understanding of yourself, of God, and your relationship with God?

2. We just learned that we were saved to enjoy God above all other things in life. What are some things in your life that stand in the way of that?

3. What do you think about the statement that a Christian's primary problem is not unbelief, but busyness? What are some practical things you could do to keep your enjoyment of God strong?

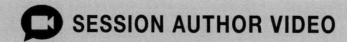 **SESSION AUTHOR VIDEO**

Watch the SESSION 2 - *SAVED FOR* author video

TrueIdentityStudy.com/walking-ti-videos-audio

REMCO BROMMET
Remco gives an overview of Session 2 - *Saved For,* along with a personal example.

🚶 WALKING IT HOME

Break into groups of 2-3

APPLYING WHAT YOU HAVE LEARNED

Discuss ways you can take what you discussed in answer to **Question 3** in **Group Discussion Questions** to create a daily and/or weekly plan to reorder your life and build in ways to enjoy the presence of God.

Type or write your plan and display it in a central place. If you have a family, discuss it with them, get their input and their help in making the enjoyment of God a priority in your weekly schedule. Commit to pray for one another during the week as you implement your plan.

 **PRAYING IT FORWARD**

Stay in small groups.

Pray for each other to be captivated anew by God's love shown to us in Christ's death on the cross. Pray for the Father to ignite a new desire in your heart to know Him and enjoy His presence, and to help you make that a priority in your daily life.

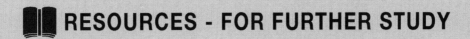

RESOURCES - FOR FURTHER STUDY

RECOMMENDED BOOKS:
Desiring God - *by Dr. John Piper*
Delighting in God - *by A.W. Tozer*
Life of the Beloved - *by Henri Nouwen*
When I Don't Desire God - by *Dr. John Piper*

SALVATION GRAPHIC
This diagram represents how and why we are saved. The great chasm of sin that separates us from God has been overcome by the death and resurrection of Jesus Christ. As we acknowledge our need to be reconciled to God and come to Him in repentance and surrender, He responds by granting us forgiveness and redemption, which includes the gift of righteousness, and adoption as His children. That opens the door for us to live a new life in of dependence on and delight in Him, and for His fullness to indwell us through the Holy Spirit.

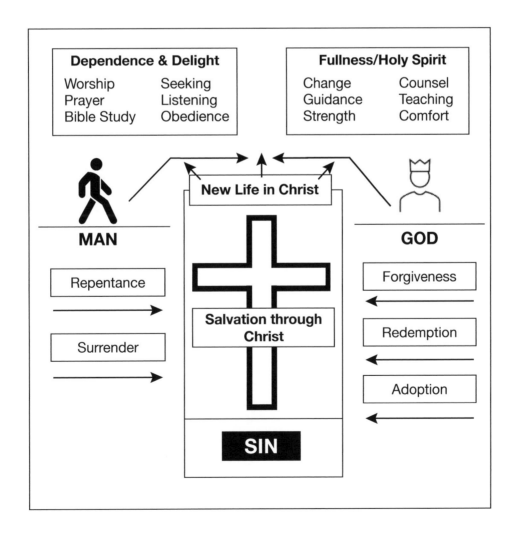

NOTES

Session 3

Intimacy with God

JUDY MILLS

*"Here I am! I stand at the door and knock. If anyone hears my voice and opens the door,
I will come in to him and eat with him, and he with me."*
Revelation 3:2

Now that we have established what we were saved from and saved for, and that glorifying God by enjoying Him forever is a major aspect of His design for us, we move on to the first of several practical ways in which delight in God and walking in your true identity becomes a daily reality: Intimacy with God.

 **SELF STUDY**

NOTE: Be sure to complete the Self Study, Core Principles, and Reflection Questions BEFORE you meet with your group each session.

God's invitation and desire for intimacy with the people He created spans the Bible:

In **Genesis 1:26-31, 3:8**, we see God seek time with Adam and Eve. He pursues a relationship with them, wanting to partner in the oversight and care of the earth alongside them.

In **Exodus 6:1-8** and **Deuteronomy 7:6-8**, we hear God's plea for a people He can call His own. A people to whom He reveals Himself through His presence and power.

In **Isaiah 5:1-2**, God speaks about a vineyard — an illustration of His longing for a people to whom He can provide and tenderly care by planting them in a land He lovingly prepared.

In the gospels (see **Matthew 1:23**), we see God come to earth as a man: Emmanuel — God with us, because He longs to reveal Himself to us.

In **Matthew 11:28-29** (NASB), we read the words of this God-man inviting us to come close — to yoke (attach, unite) ourselves to Him, to receive life from Him. Jesus said, *"Come to me, all you who are weary and burdened, and I will give you rest. Take my yoke upon you and learn from me, for I am gentle and humble in heart, and you will find rest for your souls. For my yoke is easy and, my burden is light."*

In **Philippians 3:7-8**, God reveals the intimacy He desires with us through a man named Paul. Once a persecutor of Christians, he grew to consider everything a loss in comparison to the priceless privilege of having an intimate relationship with Jesus.

And in the book of Revelation, Jesus calls to a people who fail to see their need of Him. A people He still diligently pursues: *"Here I am! I stand at the door and knock. If anyone hears my voice and opens the door, I will come in and eat with that person, and they with me."* (**Revelation 3:20**) (NIV)

God invites us to *"come closer."* He wants us to know Him deeply and share an intimate relationship with Him. He longs for us to learn and experience how He personally loves and cares for us. And through such a relationship, He seeks to establish our true identity in us.

Continue your self study with the Core Principles below. Pray and ask the Lord to reveal any new insights, understanding or personal application. Look up all Scripture verses to become more familiar with where they are in your Bible, and make notes.

 CORE PRINCIPLES

1. You Have the Priceless Privilege of Intimately Knowing God

Have you considered the incredible privilege to which God invites you, the profundity of God's invitation and pursuit of you? If someone you admire, possibly a political leader, celebrity, or church leader invited you into their innermost circle — to know everything about them and be known by them — how would you respond? Wouldn't you quickly say "Yes!" and then reorder your priorities and schedule to engage with them fully?

How much more eagerly and diligently should we respond to God?

Almighty God!
The One who made the heavens and earth (**Genesis 1:1**).

The God who lives in unapproachable light (**1 Timothy 6:16**).

The One whose hand and strength nothing can thwart or hinder (**Daniel 4:25**).

The Good Shepherd, who lovingly and thoroughly cares for His sheep (**Psalm 23**).

This God, your God, wants an intimate relationship with you. This very moment He is pursuing it with you.

The Apostle Paul understood the privilege: *"I consider everything a loss compared to the surpassing worth of knowing Christ Jesus my Lord, for whose sake I have lost all things. I consider them garbage, that I may gain Christ and be found in him."* (**Philippians 3:8-9a**)(NIV)

Yet, our response to such an invitation is often lack-luster. We may not believe God wants such a relationship with us, or we may see little value in it.

We Pursue Intimacy with God by Faith

Through this study, you will learn practical ways to come closer to God and nurture an intimate relationship with Him. But first, let us establish this principle: We pursue intimacy with God by faith:

- Believing God wants it with you.

- Believing it is of utmost importance.

- Believing you will have it.

Consider God's words in **Jeremiah 29:13-14a** (NASB): *"'You will seek Me and find Me when you search for Me with all your heart. I will be found by you,' declares the Lord."*

These words were written to a people in captivity. I am sure their circumstances made God feel very distant and disinterested in them. But He wasn't. He never is!

Do you believe God wants an intimate relationship with you?

Do you believe if you seek Him, you will indeed find him?

Do you believe a pursuit of God is worth it?

Do you believe you'll find the life and soul-peace you search for through it?

Let God reveal any unbelief.

My journey into intimacy with God began many years ago. It started with the lie that God didn't want an intimate relationship with me. I thought it was saved for an elite few, a group to which I wasn't invited.

The discovery that the invitation was for everyone was life-changing for me. It sparked a passion that continues today — nearly 30 years later. Yet, at times I struggle to prioritize it, revealing unbelief that an intimate relationship with God is worth any sacrifice needed to pursue it.

The battle in our Christian life is often one against unbelief. And because the devil hates and fears your intimacy with God (and the power released through it), his lies about it are numerous. Uncovering the lie(s) you believe and letting God bring you to a place of faith is vital in this journey

Intimacy Releases the Power of God

Intimacy is not only God's desire but His chosen method by which to pour out His power in and through us.   The word "know" in Scripture (used in the verses below) refers not only to a knowledge about God but to an experience of God — an experience of who He is and that what He says is true. He invites us to come closer to Him to experience His fullness.

- **In coming closer, we experience God's life in us.**

   Jesus said: *"And this is eternal life, that they know you, the only true God, and Jesus Christ, whom you have sent."* **(John 17:3)**. Eternal life refers not only to unending years with God in heaven (as amazing as that will be) but to an experience of the life of Christ in us now. As the verse states, we experience the life of God in us as we know Him and come into an intimate relationship with Him.

- **In coming closer, we are equipped to live a godly life.**

   According to **2 Peter 1:3** (NIV), *"His divine power has given us everything we need for a godly life through our knowledge of Him who called us by His own glory and goodness."* Everything you need to live a godly life flows from your intimacy with God.

- **In coming closer, we find peace.**

   Who doesn't struggle with some level of anxiety and unrest? Yet this too is met by God through intimacy with Him. Consider the words of **Matthew 11:28-29** in the <u>Amplified Bible Classic Edition</u>:

   "Come to Me, all you who labor and are heavy-ladened and overburdened, and I will cause you to rest. [I will ease and relieve and refresh your souls.] Take My yoke upon you and learn of Me, for I am gentle [meek] and humble [lowly] in heart, and you will find rest [relief and ease and refreshment and recreation and blessed quiet] for your souls."

- **In coming closer, God reveals the hope we have in Him, our inheritance as His people, and the incredible power that resides in us.**

  In **Ephesians 1:17-20** (NIV), the Apostle Paul prays an incredible prayer while also stating what an intimate knowledge of God releases: *"I keep asking that the God of our Lord Jesus Christ, the glorious Father, may give you the Spirit of wisdom and revelation, so that you may know Him better. I pray that the eyes of your heart may be enlightened in order that you may know the hope to which He has called you, the riches of His glorious inheritance in His holy people, and His incomparably great power for us who believe. That power is the same as the mighty strength He exerted when He raised Christ from the dead and seated Him at His right hand in the heavenly realms."*

- **In coming closer, we are filled with the fullness of God.**

  Through intimacy, we grow in a knowledge of God's love. We gain revelation of how He sees us and the new identity He's given us.

  "I pray that out of His glorious riches He may strengthen you with power through His Spirit in your inner being, so that Christ may dwell in your hearts through faith. And I pray that you, being rooted and established in love, may have power, together with all the Lord's holy people, to grasp how wide and long and high and deep is the love of Christ, and to know this love that surpasses knowledge—that you may be filled to the measure of all the fullness of God. Now to Him who is able to do immeasurably more than all we ask or imagine, according to His power that is at work within us." **Ephesians 3:16-20** (NIV)

What an astounding promise! Through our intimate, experiential knowledge of God's love, we are "filled to the measure of all the fullness of God." This truth sheds a brighter light on the verses above! Having put His Spirit in us, God wants to permeate our entire being — spirit, soul (mind, will, and emotions) and body — with His Spirit.

"May God himself, the God of peace, sanctify you through and through. May your whole spirit, soul and body be kept blameless at the coming of our Lord Jesus Christ." **1 Thessalonians 5:23** (NIV)

SOUL
* Mind
* Emotions
* Will

BODY

And if this promise seems too big, let the following verse **1 Thessalonians 5:24** (NIV) increase your faith: *"The One who calls you is faithful, and He will do it."*

As we come close to God, growing in intimacy with Him, we not only gain head knowledge about Him, but we experience Him. Under challenging circumstances, we have peace. When uncertain about what to do, He gives wisdom. When struggling to obey, He gives us His strength.

We experience that in Him is life (**John 1:4**). He becomes our life (**Colossians 3:4**)! The most important and valuable thing we do for our family, friends, co-workers, and fellow believers is seek God and nurture intimacy with God. As we know Him, as we behold Him, we become more like Him (**2 Corinthians 3:18**).

In our next session, you will learn more about hearing from God. Intimacy with Him not only is the way we enjoy His presence, it also brings us into such a close relationship with Him that we can hear Him speak to us and reveal Himself to us.

James 4:8 tells us: *"Draw near to God, and He will draw near to you."* Drawing near, coming closer, intimacy with God, are prerequisites to hear from Him.

† REFLECTION QUESTIONS

1. Write a letter to God, sharing your thoughts and emotions concerning intimacy with Him. Express your concerns, struggles, lack of desire, the joy you experience and passion you have for it.   Be honest with Him, and in doing so, give yourself the gift of acknowledging what is in your heart.

2. In what practical ways can you pursue intimacy with God?

3. We discussed how lies greatly hinder our pursuit of God. Which lie does Satan most often use on you?

How might you combat that lie?

4. What area(s) of power would you like to experience from your intimacy with God?

5. Drawing from your above answers, write a prayer to God expressing the desires of your heart.

Prayer
Pray the prayer you wrote in question 5 back to God out loud as an expression of your desire to be intimate with God.

GROUP DISCUSSION QUESTIONS

1. There is so much to learn from the Apostle Paul. Read the following passages and discuss his journey and the nature of his intimacy with God.

    Acts 8:1-3

    Acts 9:1-9

    Philippians 3:4-11

    Philippians 1:21

2. Consider that the same Holy Spirit Who lived in Paul resides in you. What would you like to pursue and believe God for in your walk of intimacy with Him?

3. What lie(s) hinder(s) you from believing or receiving intimacy with God?

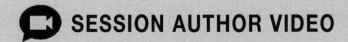
SESSION AUTHOR VIDEO

Watch the SESSION 3 - *INTIMACY WITH GOD* author video

TrueIdentityStudy.com/walking-ti-videos-audio

JUDY MILLS
Judy gives an overview of Session 3 - *Intimacy with God,* along with a personal example.

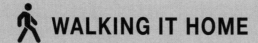
WALKING IT HOME

APPLYING WHAT YOU HAVE LEARNED

Divide into groups of 3-4.

When you ponder "that you may be filled to the measure of all the fullness of God" through your intimacy with God, how will such a filling enable you to walk and live freely in your true identity?

PRAYING IT FORWARD

Stay in small groups

Drawing from the letters and prayer you wrote to God in your Personal Reflection, or new insights gained through the group discussion, spend time in prayer, petitioning God for each other. (It may be time effective to have each person pray their request themselves, and then allow for 1-2 others to agree with them in prayer.)

📖 RESOURCES - FOR FURTHER STUDY

RECOMMENDED BOOKS:
The Ultimate Joy: A Journey in Intimacy with God - *by Judy Mills*
Drawing Near: A Life of Intimacy with God - *by John Bevere*
Experiencing God: Knowing and Doing the Will of God - *Henry Blackaby*
Prayer: Experiencing Awe and Intimacy with God - *by Timothy Keller*
Waiting on God - *by Andrew Murray*

Suggested devotional books to use in your time with God:
Awaken: 90 Days with the God who Speaks – *by Priscilla Shirer*
Daily in Christ – *by Neil Anderson*
My Utmost for His Highest – *by Oswald Chambers*
New Morning Mercies: A Daily Gospel Devotional - *by Paul David Tripp*
The Chosen - 40 Days with Jesus - *by Amanda Jenkins, Kristen Hendricks & Dallas Jenkins*
The Songs of Jesus - *by Timothy Keller* (A year of daily devotions in the Psalms)

Christian Fiction
For those who are encouraged in their faith through stories, Christian fiction and historical Christian fiction books can be a wonderful way of revealing God's truth, help bolster your faith, and open your eyes to God's love in new ways. Some are based on Bible characters and stories and others in a variety of settings and situations, giving illustration of faith in action in the ups and downs of life. Your local library may have several Christian fiction authors.

Here are a few suggested books and authors:
(For a more exhaustive list by genre, visit Christianbook.com)

Wanda E. Brunstetter - Several in an Amish Setting
Jack Cavanaugh & Bill Bright - The Great Awakening Series (1-4)
Lori Copeland
Laura K. Denton
Irene Hannon
Jan Karon - The Mitford Series
Karen Kingsbury - Several series, some based around historical events
Tim LaHaye and Jerry B. Jenkins - Left Behind Series
Beverly Lewis - Several in an Amish setting
C.S. Lewis - Chronicles of Narnia
Judith Pella - Primarily historical Christian fiction - The Russians, Ribbons West
Michael Phillips - Primarily historical Christian Fiction - Several series
A Rift in Time/Hidden in Time, The Russians, Secrets of the Shetlands, American Dreams, Caledonia series
Francine Rivers - Christian fiction and historical Christian fiction
Redeeming Love, Mark of the Lion Series, A Lineage of Grace: Biblical Stories of 5 Women in the Lineage of Jesus
Joel C. Rosenberg - Suspense & Intrigue

HAVING A QUIET TIME
by Judy Mills

God invites us to spend one on one time with Him every day!

Often referred to as a quiet time, generations of Christians testify to the profound ways in which their relationship with God was nurtured by meeting with God in the pages of the Bible daily.

Yet how to have a quiet time can be confusing. The beauty is, there are many different ways. Over time you will discover what works best for you. Below are two options if you'd like some direction or are looking for new methods and practices to incorporate into your time of encountering with God through His Word.

TWO METHODS TO CONSIDER

SOAP method
This method is thoroughly explained on a website called *Love God Greatly*:
https://lovegodgreatly.com/how-to-soap/

> The title is an acronym:
> **S** - Scripture
> **O** - Observation
> **A** - Application
> **P** - Prayer

S: You begin by writing out the **Scripture** passage. This exercise slows down your mind and allows God to highlight specific words or phrases.

O: In the **observation** phase, consider the original audience, the context in which it's written, and notice any repetitive words or phrases. Note again what words or phrases stand out to you. Let this phase be fun — God is leading you to discover truths He has for you.

A: In the **application** phase, God's Word becomes personal. Ask questions such as: *"What is God saying to me? How can I apply this to my life?"*

P: Pray God's Word back to Him. If you've sensed God calling you to a specific action, into confession, or revealing a part of His character to you — *pray it all.*

Recently I was reading **Psalm 42:1-2** (TLB), *"As the deer pants for water, so I long for you, O God. I thirst for God, the living God. Where can I find Him to come and stand before Him?"*

On that morning, I didn't feel a great longing for God. So, *praying* His Word, I asked God for the desire.

LECTIO DIVINA method

Lectio Divina means divine reading. This method is an ancient monastic practice, and it too has four steps.

1. **Lectio (Read)** - Slowly read the Scripture passage, noting what words or phrases catch your attention.

2. **Meditatio (Reflect)** - Read through the passage a second time, focusing further on what stood out to you. Meditate on those words and phrases, noting what thoughts or ideas come to your mind about them.

3. **Oratio (Respond/Pray)** - Now, talk to God about your observations. I journal these thoughts and ideas so I don't forget them later.

4. **Contemplatio (Rest/Contemplate)** - Allow 5-10 minutes (you can start with just a minute or two and work up to more) to sit quietly and allow God to speak. For many of us, our mind wanders, especially at first. If it does, simply redirect your mind back to God.

These two websites describe the Lectio Divina method:
https://bustedhalo.com/ministry-resources/lectio-divina-beginners-guide
https://www.faithward.org/lectio-divina-an-ancient-contemplative-spiritual-practice/)

Any new practice takes time. Spending time with God will be no different. Just keep showing up! The websites listed give a more thorough explanation of these two methods and may help you determine if one or a combination of the two ways works best for you.

My time alone with God is the most life-giving thing I do each day. I have my quiet time first thing in the morning when I'm less distracted and better able to focus on God. Since I love all things cozy and pretty, I always have a soft blanket, warm fire or candle, and a big cup of coffee to accompany my Bible and journal. My journal is where I write my prayers to God and record any words or insights I sense Him revealing to me.

I encourage you to arrange the time and space in a manner that blesses you. One of my friends has her quiet time outside whenever the weather permits. Nature draws her closer to God. Some people find it helpful to open their quiet time with a worship song. Some begin with a short devotion to focus their thoughts on God. Others find standing or kneeling helps direct their gaze to God. Experiment with different environments and methods.

Above all, know how completely delighted God is with your desire and the effort you make to spend time with Him. Even when I don't "feel" God, I know by faith that He is with me. I know He's heard me. I know He sees the time as an offering to Him and evidence of my desire to know Him.

God is waiting to spend time with you!

NOTES

Session 4

Hearing From God

DEBBIE JONES

"So then faith comes by hearing, and hearing by the word of God."
Romans 10:17 (NKJV)

One of the greatest privileges of intimacy with God, and one of the most important keys to knowing and walking in your true identity is hearing from God. You have already had some practice with that in the *True Identity Study* when you learned to listen to the Lord speak to you through some of your personal reflection times. (See page 5-6 in the *True Identity Study Guide.*)

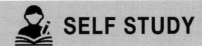

SELF STUDY

NOTE: Be sure to complete the Self Study, Core Principles, and Reflection Questions BEFORE you meet with your group each session.

As children of God, we can hear from our heavenly Father. His Word declares that to be true in **John 10**. The verse from Romans above explains that our faith grows as we hear from God, and that it is knowing the Word of God which enables us to discern that it is God we are hearing. Relationship is built on good communication, two-way communication. God is speaking, are we listening?

Continue your self study with the Core Principles below. Pray and ask the Lord to reveal any new insights, understanding or personal application. Look up all Scripture verses to become more familiar with where they are in your Bible, and make notes.

⊶ CORE PRINCIPLES

1. *All God's Children Can Hear Him When He Speaks*

Our God is all about relationship, so He is also all about communication, two-way communication. There are many examples in the Bible and the first is found in Genesis, the Book of Beginnings, according to the Hebrew title. God walked with Adam and Eve in the cool of the day (**Genesis 3:8**), and He wants to do the same with you (**Leviticus 26:12**).

What do you think God was discussing with Adam and Eve?

Well, what do you discuss with your family or friends at the end of your day?

Do you think God wants to hear from you at the end of the day?

What are some things you might share with Him?

John 10 speaks of the shepherd whose sheep know his voice and follow him. Jesus is our shepherd and we are the sheep of His pasture. He speaks and by the presence of the Holy Spirit in us, we know it is Him. Are you listening for Him?

2. *God Has Given Us a Spirit Which is Empowered by the Holy Spirit to Receive Spiritual Things*

We are three-part beings (**1 Thessalonians 5:23**) – body, soul (mind, will and emotions) and spirit. The body is the "receiver" and "processor" of the natural realm, the soul is the receiver and processor of psychological matters, and the spirit is the receiver and processor of the spiritual realm. Jesus has given us the Holy Spirit which empowers our spirit. He serves us in many ways – as counselor, helper, comforter, teacher. He imparts gifts to us to use in service to others and to bring glory to God.

Jesus said to His disciples in **Acts 1:8** -
"But you will receive power when the Holy Spirit has come upon you, and you will be my witnesses in Jerusalem and in all Judea and Samaria, and to the end of the earth."

1 Corinthians 2:13-14 (AMP) tells us -
"We also speak of these things, not in words taught or supplied by human wisdom, but in those taught by the Spirit, combining and interpreting spiritual thoughts with spiritual words [for those being guided by the Holy Spirit]. But the natural [unbelieving] man does not accept the things [the teachings and revelations] of the Spirit of God, for they are foolishness [absurd and illogical] to him; and he is incapable of understanding them, because they are spiritually discerned and appreciated, [and he is unqualified to judge spiritual matters]."

And from **Hebrews 4:12** (TPT) –
"For we have the living Word of God, which is full of energy, and it pierces more sharply than a two-edged sword. It will even penetrate to the very core of our being where soul and spirit, bone and marrow meet! It interprets and reveals the true thoughts and secret motives of our hearts."

3. *What God Speaks to You is Always in Agreement with His Nature, His Character and His Word*

We live in the information age. Facts are at our fingertips as we surf the Internet. But facts are not truth. There is only one truth and that is Jesus Christ. Anything that contradicts Him and His word is not truth. The enemy will attempt to deceive you – that is in his job description. However, God has made provisions for us through the Holy Spirit, so that we will not be deceived. **1 John 2:18-27** assures us that because we are anointed by the Holy One, we know truth. Truth is a person, it is Jesus. He is the one who lives in us and speaks to us. Therefore, what we hear must be in agreement with Him – His nature, His character and His word. The Holy Spirit will help us to know that what we hear comes from God.

In **John 16:12-13** (TPT) Jesus tells His disciples –
"There is so much more I would like to say to you, but it's more than you can grasp at this moment. But when the truth-giving Spirit comes, he will unveil the reality of every truth within you. He won't speak his own message, but only what he hears from the Father, and he will reveal prophetically to you what is to come."

4. *God Speaks to His Children in Different Ways*

Our God is very creative, just look around you at His creation, there is so much variety, color, majesty, beauty. His communication with His children is just as varied. He "speaks" to us in dreams, visions, pictures, words, Scripture, impressions, feelings, a sense of His presence, other people.

As we become more aware of His presence, we become more aware of His communication with us. Likewise, as we seek Him, He promises that we will find Him when we seek Him with all our heart. Sometimes the seeking becomes like a treasure hunt. We ask, He answers but in His perfect timing, in His perfect way.

Proverbs 25:2 (NIV) says –
"It is the glory of God to conceal a matter; to search out a matter is the glory of kings."

And **The Passion Translation** says it this way –
"God conceals the revelation of his word in the hiding place of his glory. But the honor of kings is revealed by how they thoroughly search out the deeper meaning of all that God says."

God has told us in His word to ask, seek and knock. He invites us to find Him, to know Him and to be known by Him. Our relationship with Him is based on communication with Him, two way communication.

✝ REFLECTION QUESTIONS

As mentioned in the Introduction, it is recommended that as you go through this study, you keep a journal of your communications with God.

1. Read the passage below from **1 John** with the help of the Holy Spirit. Ask Him to reveal to you what you need to know. Mark the words or phrases that the Holy Spirit highlights for you. In your journal, write down what comes to your mind as you read and meditate on this passage of Scripture. If you lack understanding, ask the Holy Spirit to open up the Word to you.

   1 John 2:20-21(TPT)
   "But the Holy One has anointed you and you all know the truth. So I'm writing you not because you don't know the truth, but because you do know it, and no lie belongs to the truth."

   The Power of the Truth

   1 John 2:22-25 (TPT)
   "Who is the real liar but the one who denies that Jesus is the Christ. He is the real anti-christ, the one who denies the Father and the Son. Whoever rejects the Son rejects the Father. Whoever embraces the Son embraces the Father also. So you must be sure to keep the message burning in your hearts; that is, the message of life you heard from the beginning. If you do, you will always be living in close fellowship with the Son and with the Father. And he himself has promised us the never-ending life of the ages to come!"

   1 John 2:26-27 (TPT)
   "I've written these things about those who are attempting to lead you astray. But the wonderful anointing you have received from God is so much greater than their deception and now lives in you. There's no need for anyone to keep teaching you. His anointing teaches you all that you need to know, for it will lead you into truth, not a counterfeit. So, just as the anointing has taught you, remain in him."

2. The passage from **1 John** says that we have been anointed by the Holy One. Look up anointing and write down the definition.

   Who is the Holy One?

   Why do you think we have been anointed?

   What does this anointing have to do with knowing truth?

   Find another passage in Scripture that speaks about anointing. Does the passage help you to understand this passage from 1 John better? Explain.

3. Look at what God revealed to you about the passage from 1 John. How does His revelation to you agree with His nature, His character and His word?

4. How did God speak to you about this passage (words, Scripture, pictures, etc.)?

How does He normally communicate with you?

Is there anything you would like for Him to change about His communication with you?

Is there anything you would like to change about your communication with Him?

What would you like for God to reveal to you about Himself?

About you?

What would you like to ask Him?

Prayer
"Dear Father, thank you that you are a God who speaks to us in so many ways. I confess that at times I am uncertain about hearing from an unseen God. Help me to recognize your voice speaking to me through your Word and to my spirit. Help me to make room in my heart, my life and my home for you to speak. I would very much like to know you better and ask that you reveal yourself to me. I would also like to see myself, the people in my life, and the world as whole through your perspective. So help me be still, listen, understand, and see through your eyes. In Jesus' Name ~ Amen."

👥 GROUP DISCUSSION QUESTIONS

1. Why do you think it is important to hear from God?

2. Read some of these verses and compare them to your answer to question one.

   2 Kings 17:13-15

   Proverbs 1:5

   Isaiah 55:2-3

   Isaiah 55:8-9

   Isaiah 55:10-11

   Amos 3:7

   Luke 10:38-40

3. What do you think God wants to say to you? What do you think He wants to say to others through you?

4. How would you explain to someone that you hear from God?

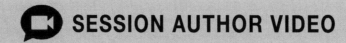

Watch the SESSION 4 - *HEARING FROM GOD* author video

<u>TrueIdentityStudy.com/walking-ti-videos-audio</u>

DEBBIE JONES

Debbie gives an overview of Session 4 - *Hearing from God,* along with a personal example.

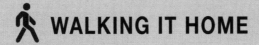

WALKING IT HOME

APPLYING WHAT YOU HAVE LEARNED

GROUP ACTIVITY

Divide into groups of three.

Each person asks the Lord for a number between 1 and 150, and then reads the Psalm that corresponds to that number.

After reading, ask the Lord what He wants you to know about the Psalm and how it applies to you particularly; share what you have heard with your group for their confirmation.

 **PRAYING IT FORWARD**

Stay in small groups

Pray for each other based on what the Lord revealed during the "Walking it Home" activity, that God would help you apply the insights you received in your life.

_____
_____
_____
_____
_____
_____
_____
_____
_____
_____
_____
_____
_____
_____
_____
_____
_____
_____
_____
_____
_____
_____
_____
_____

📖 RESOURCES - FOR FURTHER STUDY

RECOMMENDED BOOKS

How to Hear God's Voice - *by Mark and Patti Virkler*
The Word Speaks – *by Lucius J. Malcolm, Forward by Dr. Mark Virkler*
F. B. Meyer article *How To Read Your Bible* and related information:
https://www.path2prayer.com/

STEPS TO HEAR FROM GOD (See page 5 in the *True Identity Study Guide*)

1. Quiet Yourself
2. Focus on the Lord
3. Listen/watch for His answer

4. Write down what God brings to your mind
5. Weigh what you have written against God's Word, His nature and His character.

From ***The Word For You Today***
October 26

John 10:4
"When he has brought out all his own, he goes before them, and the sheep follow him, for they know his voice."

IT IS IMPORTANT TO ADOPT THE PRACTICE OF HEARING FROM GOD FIRST!

Hearing from God before *you entertain the ideas of others.*
Their ideas are not His commands. Don't make commitments and end up bound by promises you can't keep.

Hearing from God before *you listen to the complaints of others.*
You are not responsible for their happiness. The need to fix others to feel good about yourself is a sign of codependency.

Hearing from God before *you consider the needs of others.*
Their needs are driving them. Only the plan of God should be leading you.

Hearing from God before *you respond to the requests of others.*
You must discern what's behind their requests. Check the soil before you sow your seed.

Hearing from God before *you share your dream with others.*
It's not enough to have a dream, you must have a team. You need people to help you, cheer you on and lift you to a higher level. The right people motivate you to grow stronger, think better, work harder and risk more. They compel you to continue.

Hearing from God before *you seek the approval of others.*
People with an agenda will flatter and manipulate you. Hearing God's voice will keep you from falling into their trap.

Hearing from God before *you make significant changes.*
It's not your job to decide what God wants you to do, but to discover what He wants and do it.

From *The Word for You Today*
January 9, 2014

THE BIBLE IS GOD SPEAKING TO YOU

John 6:63 (ESV)
"It is the Spirit who gives life; the flesh is no help at all. The words that I have spoken to you are spirit and life."

Did you know that the longest telegraphic message ever dispatched was in May, 1881? It carried 188,000 words. It was printed in full that day in the Chicago Times. One of the nation's leading newspapers gave space for four Gospels, the Acts of the Apostles, and the Epistle to the Romans. 'A triumph of publicity' was the verdict of the nation's press.

All this was done because the Revised Version of the New Testament in English was on sale that day in New York City, thirty-three thousand copies were sold within twenty-four hours, setting a new sales record for any book.

Why does the Bible remain the world's most widely read book? For one simple reason: you read every other book – the Bible reads you!

You say, *"But I don't get a lot out of the Bible when I read it."* You are not alone; many people say the same thing. But it doesn't have to be that way.

"Read the Bible not as a newspaper, but as a love letter. If a cluster of heavenly fruit hangs within your reach, gather it. If a promise lies upon the page as a blank check, cash it. If a prayer is recorded, launch it as a feathered arrow from the bow of your desire." F. B. Meyer

Why do we keep going back to the Bible? Because in a world where trust is in short supply, *"Not one word has failed of all the good promises He gave."*

The Letter of St. James - December 17, 2020
St. James Church, Athens, Georgia

No Doubt About It
by Mike Cantrell

The Apostle James wrote something quite challenging:

"If any of you lacks wisdom, he should ask God, who gives generously to all without finding fault, and it will be given to him. But when he asks, he must believe and not doubt, because he who doubts is like a wave of the sea, blown and tossed by the wind."

We often come to crossroads in life. Times when we need wisdom. Is it possible to receive wisdom from God and not doubt? That is a challenge indeed. Yet, this is the way of faith.

When I am at a crossroad, this helps me: rather than trying to decide which path to take, my goal is to discern God's will and then choose to be obedient. There is much freedom in this way of knowing which path to take.

It took me quite a few years to learn not to doubt. The key for me was realizing that I had been putting my faith in my weak ability to hear rather than in God's ability to speak clearly. My faith was in myself, not in Him. He knows how to break through my weaknesses. Now, I put my faith in Him and His promises, not in my abilities.

He promises to give you wisdom when you ask. If you don't have the wisdom you seek, then you don't need it right now. God will give you the wisdom you need when you need it. Do not doubt that. It's His promise to you.

NOTES

Session 5

The Holy Spirit In You

REMCO BROMMET

*"If you love me you will keep my commandments. And I will ask the Father,
and He will give you another Helper, to be with you forever, even the Spirit of truth,
whom the world cannot receive, because it neither sees Him nor knows Him.
You know Him, for He dwells with you and will be in you."*
John 14:15-17

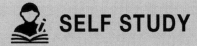 **SELF STUDY**

***NOTE: Be sure to complete the Self Study, Core Principles, and Reflection Questions
BEFORE you meet with your group each session.***

One of the things you discovered in the *True Identity Study* is the importance of knowing who you are in Christ and who Christ is in you. To know who Christ is in you, it is vital to understand the person and work of the Holy Spirit: He is the One who lives in us. Yet for many believers, that is an unfamiliar idea.

Former mega-church pastor and author Frances Chan agrees. In his book, <u>The Forgotten God</u>, he notes that many faithful, churchgoing believers still ask the question, *"I've got Jesus, why do I need the Holy Spirit?"*

What does the Bible tell us? Who is the Holy Spirit? We will answer these questions in this session.

Continue your self study with the Core Principles below. Pray and ask the Lord to reveal any new insights, understanding or personal application. Look up all Scripture verses to become more familiar with where they are in your Bible, and make notes.

CORE PRINCIPLES

1. *The Holy Spirit is the Third Person of the Trinity*

We are triune beings – body, soul (mind, will and emotions), and spirit, and we are created in the image of God who is Himself triune – Father, Son and Holy Spirit. Three distinct persons with distinct functions, and yet completely one in substance, heart and mind.

The Holy Spirit –

- Is God, not merely a messenger (see **1 Corinthians 3:16**, **2 Corinthians 3:17**)

- Is a person, not a force (see **John 14:26**, **Romans 8:16**)

- Has a mind, a will and emotions (see **Romans 8:27** and **15:30**, **1 Corinthians 12:11**, **Ephesians 4:30**)

The Holy Spirit was also:

- Present and involved in the Creation (**Genesis 1:2**)

- Revealed God's mind to the prophets (**Acts 2:18, 1 Peter 1:21**)

- Anointed and empowered God's servants (**Luke 4:18**)

- Connected Jesus to God during His days here on earth (**Matthew 3:16-17**)

- Poured out upon believers in place of Christ's physical presence (**John 16:7, Acts 2:4, 10:44-45**).

The Holy Spirit Lives in Us

In his book, _Experiencing the Holy Spirit_, Andrew Murray says, *"Through the Holy Spirit we receive the fullness of God to indwell us."*

When we repented and gave our hearts to Christ, the Holy Spirit came to live in us. The Bible calls that being "born again" or "being born from above." (**John 3:3-5**).

We experience the fullness of God as we trust that the Holy Spirit lives in us to change us from the inside out so that we are set free to live in our true identity. True freedom is that we do not have to strive in our own strength to become who God created us to be, but rather allowing the Holy Spirit to change us from the inside out. This is what the Apostle Paul means when he says in **Philippians 2:13** *"...for it is God who works in you, both to will and to work for His good pleasure."*

The Holy Spirit fulfills a variety of roles in us and for us. Some are described in Jesus' announcement of His coming and some in the writings of the apostles.

- He indwells us (**John 20:21-23**, **Romans 8:9**, **1 Corinthians 6:19-20**)

- He teaches us (**John 14:26, 16:13-15**)

- He convicts us of sin (**John 16:8**)

- He empowers us as He did Jesus (**Luke 4: 14**, **Acts 1:8**, **1 Corinthians 12:11**)

- He guides and directs us (**Acts 16:6-7**)

- He transforms us (**Romans 8:11**, **2 Corinthians 3:18**, **Galatians 5:22-23**)

- He prays for us (**Romans 8:27**)

- He seals us and guarantees our inheritance as children of God (**Ephesians 1:13-14**)

- He gives us gifts for life and ministry (**1 Corinthians 12:4-11**, **Romans 12:6-8**, **Ephesians 4:7-16**, **1 Peter 4:10-11**)

The question for many is: *"Does the Holy Spirit do all that work in me without me having to do anything at all?"* That is an important question, and the answer is, *"No!"*

Keeping in Step with The Holy Spirit

The Apostle Paul makes much of born-again believers setting their minds on, or keeping in step with, the Holy Spirit.

"There is therefore now no condemnation for those who are in Christ Jesus. For the law of the Spirit of life has set you free in Christ Jesus from the law of sin and death. For God has done what the law, weakened by the flesh, could not do. By sending his own Son in the likeness of sinful flesh and for sin, he condemned sin in the flesh, in order that the righteous requirement of the law might be fulfilled in us, who walk not according to the flesh but according to the Spirit. For those who live according to the flesh set their minds on the things of the flesh, but those who live according to the Spirit set their minds on the things of the Spirit. For to set the mind on the flesh is death, but to set the mind on the Spirit is life and peace. For the mind that is set on the flesh is hostile to God, for it does not submit to God's law; indeed, it cannot. Those who are in the flesh cannot please God.

You, however, are not in the flesh but in the Spirit, if in fact the Spirit of God dwells in you. Anyone who does not have the Spirit of Christ does not belong to him. But if Christ is in you, although the body is dead because of sin, the Spirit is life because of righteousness. If the Spirit of him who raised Jesus from the dead dwells in you, he who raised Christ Jesus from the dead will also give life to your mortal bodies through his Spirit who dwells in you." **Romans 8:1-11**

"But I say, walk by the Spirit, and you will not gratify the desires of the flesh. For the desires of the flesh are against the Spirit, and the desires of the Spirit are against the flesh, for these are opposed to each other, to keep you from doing the things you want to do. But if you are led by the Spirit, you are not under the law. Now the works of the flesh are evident: sexual immorality, impurity, sensuality, idolatry, sorcery, enmity, strife, jealousy, fits of anger, rivalries, dissensions, divisions, envy, drunkenness, orgies, and things like these. I warn you, as I warned you before, that those who do such things will not inherit the kingdom of God. But the fruit of the Spirit is love, joy, peace, patience, kindness, goodness, faithfulness, gentleness, self-control; against such things there is no law. And those who belong to Christ Jesus have crucified the flesh with its passions and desires. If we live by the Spirit, let us also keep in step with the Spirit." **Galatians 5:16-25**

According to these passages, a mind set on the Holy Spirit is the complete opposite of a mind set on the things of the flesh, i.e. our sinful human nature. The latter leads to a lifestyle filled with things abhorrent to God (see **Galatians 5:18-21**), even hostility toward God (**Romans 8:7**), as well as death and separation from God. But a mind set on the Holy Spirit leads to freedom, life, peace and fruit.

How exactly do we keep in step with the Holy Spirit?

Much of what you have learned so far in this study and in the *True identity Study*, relates to setting our minds on the Spirit. It involves a progression of four steps:

Step 1: Be intentional in ordering your daily life to make room for Him: To interact with God and pursue intimacy with Him, delight in Him and listen to Him in keeping with what you have learned in Sessions 2, 3 and 4.

Step 2: **Yield to the Holy Spirit:** Give Him full control to do His transforming work in you. A Christian lives with a healthy sense of conviction that no good indwells our fallen nature and we cannot change ourselves (**Romans 7:18**). We need the Holy Spirit to change us in the image of Christ (**Romans 8:29**).

Step 3: Listen to God: He speaks to us through His Word, applied to our lives by the Holy Spirit, Who gives us God's Truth and perspectives, and prompts us to act according to His will. We have already learned that He also opens our eyes to lies we have been believing and helps us replace them with His truths of who we are in Christ.

Step 4: Obey: Whenever God prompts us through the Holy Spirit to do something specific, repent of something, or change our behavior, we must obey in the faith that He helps us in our weakness (**Romans 8:26, Philippians 2:13**).

The Fruit of The Spirit

When we make room, yield, listen and obey, the Holy Spirit begins to bear fruit in us that makes us recognizable as followers of Jesus.

Christ made much of fruit being the outward expression of what's inside. After all, it is difficult sometimes to distinguish an apple tree from a pear tree or a peach tree until you see the fruit on the branches. In **Matthew 7:16** He uses the illustration of fruit to warn against false prophets, and in **John 15: 1-8** He describes the relationship between the vine and the branches as the key to understanding God's purpose for our lives: as we hold on to Him with all we've got, He pours out His life in us through the Holy Spirit. That in turn becomes visible in spiritual fruit so people recognize that we are His disciples by the way we live. We can't produce our own fruit. He does that in us. But we do have to hold on to Him with all our might by following step 1-4 above. If we don't, we cut ourselves off from God's life in us, we become spiritually dry, lose our fruit, and ultimately our relationship with God.

The fruit that Jesus talks about as making us recognizable as followers of Christ is described in **Galatians 5:22** as love, joy, peace, patience, kindness, goodness, faithfulness, gentleness and self-control. This is a series of mindsets and attitudes toward other people that are opposite to those of the flesh, described in vs. 18-21: sexual immorality, impurity, sensuality, idolatry, sorcery, enmity, strife, jealousy, first of anger, rivalries, dissensions, divisions, envy, drunkenness orgies, and things like these. It is a godly mindset versus a worldly mindset.

We call it fruit of the Spirit, and not fruits, because, much like an orange is made up of individual wedges that can be separated but that all look, smell and taste the same, the individual mindsets that make up the fruit of the Spirit belong together. You can't have love without kindness and patience, for instance.

The liberating miracle of being a Christian is that Christ lives in us through the Holy Spirit, and He takes full responsibility for producing that fruit in us as long as we set our minds on Him. We don't have to, and in fact cannot, manufacture the fruit of the Spirit by obeying a bunch of rules or by self-improvement.

The fruit of the spirit, much like fruit in the garden, grows steadily. In a new believer, not much of it may be visible at first. As the Holy Spirit does His work, it gradually grows and becomes fuller and riper, and outshines what remains in you of your old nature.

Visible fruit, which you may not even be aware of yourself, is evidence beyond any doubt that you are walking in your true identity, keeping in step with the Holy Spirit and that He is changing you from the inside out into who He has designed you to be!

✝ REFLECTION QUESTIONS

1. Read **John 14:15-17, 25, 26**; and **John 16:7-15**. List everything Jesus says the Holy Spirit does in you:

   Which of these things have you experienced, and how?

2. Read **Romans 7 and 8**. Romans 7 describes the reality of what it means to be enslaved to sin. It helps us understand the importance of setting our mind on the things of the Spirit to experience freedom.

   What specific sinful habits have you struggled with?

   Are any of these related to the core lies you have identified and confronted in the *True Identity Study*? If so, how?

3. Read **Galatians 5:16-25**. Which "works of the flesh" are still present in your life?

What are the mindsets from **verse 22** that are the opposite to those?

Take some time to bring what you wrote down in question 2 and 3 before the Lord in prayer.

- Confess them as sin

- Renounce them as hostile to God and worthy of complete removal

- Invite the Holy Spirit to change them from works of the flesh into fruit of the Spirit

- Reaffirm your commitment to pursue intimacy with the Father so the Holy Spirit can do His work in you.

Prayer:
"Father in heaven, I confess that I have at times misunderstood and neglected the presence and work of the Holy Spirit in me. Help me to recognize His voice more clearly, to give Him full control over my soul, and obey His promptings and direction. Grant me the willpower and dedication to make room for Him in my daily life, and make my relationship with Him a priority so that you can work in me to work and will according to your good pleasure, and bear fruit in me to your glory. In Jesus' Name ~ Amen."

GROUP DISCUSSION QUESTIONS

1. What new things did you learn in this chapter about the Holy Spirit?

    What stood out to you the most?

2. What are some warning signs that you may be walking in the flesh versus keeping in step with the Spirit?

3. In what practical ways should the various parts of the fruit of the Spirit, like love, patience, and kindness, manifest themselves in a believer's life?

4. What are the benefits of keeping in step with the Spirit versus walking in the flesh?

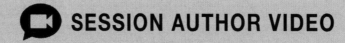

SESSION AUTHOR VIDEO

Watch the SESSION 5 - *THE HOLY SPIRIT IN YOU* author video

TrueIdentityStudy.com/walking-ti-videos-audio

REMCO BROMMET
Remco gives an overview of Session 5 - *The Holy Spirit In You,* along with a personal example.

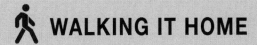

WALKING IT HOME

APPLYING WHAT YOU HAVE LEARNED

Break into groups of 2-3

The Apostle Paul sometimes closes his letters with the benediction, *"The grace of the Lord Jesus Christ and the love of God, and the fellowship of the Holy Spirit be with you all."* (**2 Corinthians 13:14**).

Discuss what the fellowship with the Holy Spirit looks like in everyday life.

What helps your fellowship and what hinders it?

 **PRAYING IT FORWARD**

Stay in your small groups

Pray for one another to have the courage and dedication to make room for the Holy Spirit, yield to His work, listen to what He is speaking, and obey His prompting and direction.

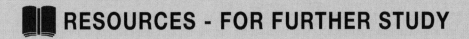

RESOURCES - FOR FURTHER STUDY

RECOMMENDED BOOKS
Fresh Wind, Fresh Fire, Fresh Faith - *by Jim Cymbala*
The Holy Spirit - *by Billy Graham*
The Helper - *by Catherine Marshall*
The Forgotten God - *by Frances Chan*
The Spirit-filled Life - *by John MacNeil*

THE TRINITY
This diagram describes our Triune God: Father, Son and Holy Spirit, who is often called the "Third Person" of the Trinity. God presents Himself as all three roles, equal in mind, substance, and power.
But the roles are distinct in nature. Therefore, the Father is not the Holy Spirit or the Son, the Son is not the Father or the Holy Spirit, and the Holy Spirit is not the Father or the Son.

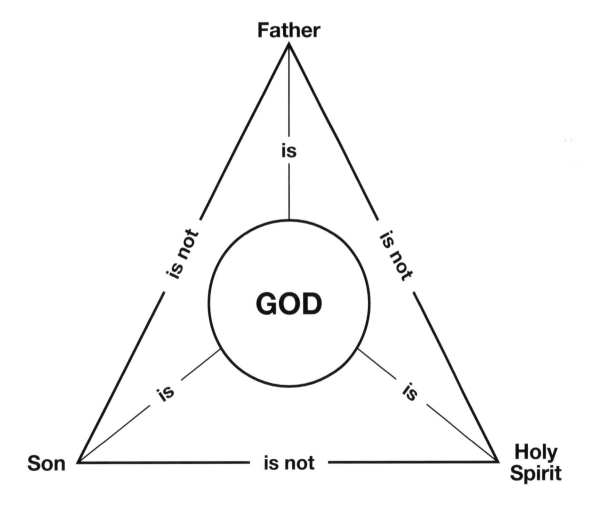

FOUR KEYS TO KEEPING IN STEP WITH THE SPIRIT

This diagram shows the four key things we have to do to keep in Step with the Holy Spirit so we will yield fruit:

- We **make room** in our daily schedule and in our hearts for Him to reveal God to us.

- We **yield** to Him in reverent acknowledgment that He changes us in the image of Christ, teaches us, empowers us, counsels us, corrects us, and gives us spiritual gifts.

- We **listen** to what He has to say to us through the written Word and through His direct promptings.

- We **obey** His promptings, instructions and corrections.

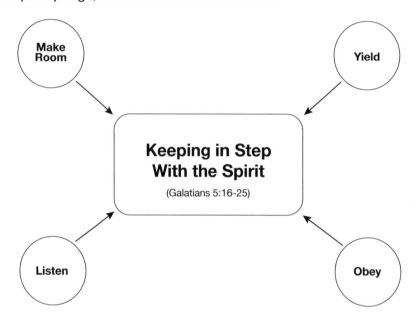

THE 3 ENVELOPES

Jennifer used the illustration of the 3 Envelopes in the *True Identity Study* when talking about **who you are in Christ** and **who Christ is in you** (the Holy Spirit in you).

The 1st envelope (the Holy Spirit) is in the 2nd envelope (You) at the same time both (1 & 2 envelope) are in the 3rd envelope (God).

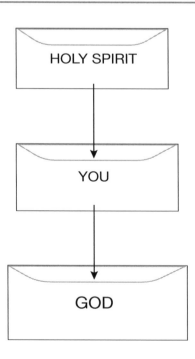

NOTES

NOTES

Session 6

DEBBIE JONES

"God has given each of you a gift from his great variety of spiritual gifts. Use them well to serve one another. Do you have the gift of speaking? Then speak as though God himself were speaking through you. Do you have the gift of helping others? Do it with all the strength and energy that God supplies. Then everything you do will bring glory to God through Jesus Christ. All glory and power to him forever and ever! Amen."
1 Peter 4:10-11 (NLT)

In the previous session, we learned more about the person and work of the Holy Spirit in us as individual believers. However, the Holy Spirit also plays a crucial role in leading and building up the worldwide community of believers, otherwise known as the Church or the Body of Christ.

 **SELF STUDY**

NOTE: Be sure to complete the Self Study, Core Principles, and Reflection Questions BEFORE you meet with your group each session.

God has seen fit in His wisdom to provide, through the Holy Spirit, spiritual gifts to every person to serve others, build each other up, accomplish the plans He has for us, and bring glory to Him. If we hide those gifts, we do ourselves, others and God a great disservice. There is Kingdom work to be done and we are an important part of God's plan.

Continue your self study with the Core Principles below. Pray and ask the Lord to reveal any new insights, understanding or personal application. Look up all Scripture verses to become more familiar with where they are in your Bible, and make notes.

⊙⊸ CORE PRINCIPLES

1. God Has Given Each One of Us a Spiritual Gift

This is clearly stated in **1 Peter 4:10-11** – God has given each one of us a spiritual gift from His great variety of gifts.

1 Corinthians 12:4-6 tells us – *"Now there are varieties of gifts, but the same Spirit; and there are varieties of service, but the same Lord; and there are varieties of activities, but it is the same God who empowers them all in everyone."* The Holy Spirit, Jesus and God the Father all work together empowering believers to perform a variety of service through the gifts given.

In **Romans 12:4-5** we are told that just like the parts of a body do not have the same function, so we as members of the body of Christ have different gifts. Our gifts are always with us; **Romans 11:29** states – *"For the gifts and the calling of God are irrevocable."*

No one has all the gifts, neither do we live or serve in isolation. We must work together as the body of Christ for all the gifts to be displayed and used for the building up of the members of the body. (See **Ephesians 4:1-16**)

Gifts Are to Be Used to Serve One Another

To each is given the manifestation of the Spirit for the common good.
(**1 Corinthians 12:7**)

Use them well to serve one another. (**1 Peter 4:10**)

Just as our bodies have many parts and each part has a special function, so it is with Christ's body. We are many parts of one body, and we all belong to each other. (**Romans 12:4-5**)

These verses let us know why we have received gifts from God – for the common good, to serve one another because we all belong to each other. In doing so, God will be glorified.

God Has Planned Good Works for Each One of Us to Do

In His Word, God tells us that He has plans for us, good works for us to do. He has gifted us to be able to accomplish His plans and purposes.

Ephesians 2:10 says – *"For we are his workmanship, created in Christ Jesus for good works, which God prepared beforehand, that we should walk in them."*

"For we are His workmanship [His own master work, a work of art], created in Christ Jesus [reborn from above—spiritually transformed, renewed, ready to be used] for good works, which God prepared [for us] beforehand [taking paths which He set], so that we would walk in them [living the good life which He prearranged and made ready for us]" (AMP)

Love Must Be the Motivation for the Use of Our Gifts

There are three primary places in Scripture where gifts are mentioned and listed – **Romans 12**, **1 Corinthians 12 and Ephesians 4**. What is interesting is what follows the verses containing the types of gifts.

Romans 12:9-13
"Let love be genuine. Abhor what is evil; hold fast to what is good. Love one another with brotherly affection. Outdo one another in showing honor. Do not be slothful in zeal, be fervent in spirit, serve the Lord. Rejoice in hope, be patient in tribulation, be constant in prayer. Contribute to the needs of the saints and seek to show hospitality."

1 Corinthians 13:1-3
"If I speak in the tongues of men and of angels, but have not love, I am a noisy gong or a clanging cymbal. And if I have prophetic powers, and understand all mysteries and all knowledge, and if I have all faith, so as to remove mountains, but have not love, I am nothing. If I give away all I have, and if I deliver up my body to be burned, but have not love, I gain nothing."

Ephesians 4:11-16
"And he gave the apostles, the prophets, the evangelists, the shepherds, and teachers, to equip the saints for the work of ministry, for building up the body of Christ, until we all attain to the unity of the faith and of the knowledge of the Son of God, to mature manhood, to the measure of the stature of the fullness of Christ, so that we may no longer be children, tossed to and fro by the waves and carried about by every wind of doctrine, by human cunning, by craftiness in deceitful schemes. Rather, speaking the truth in love, we are to grow up in every way into him who is the head, into Christ, from whom the whole body, joined and held together by every joint with which it is equipped, when each part is working properly, makes the body grow so that it builds itself up in love."

Instructions about love accompany the verses about gifts. This is no mistake; God knows that love is what identifies us to the world as disciples of Jesus.

5. Spiritual Gifts Confirmed and Matured

It is beneficial to you to have your spiritual gifts confirmed by other mature believers to give you a sense of assurance that you correctly understand what gifts you have. (See Note below)

You will mature in your spiritual gifts over time and with experience. If you have the gift of teaching, for instance, you may not become a brilliant teacher overnight. You receive the gift, and then God develops it in you through use, experience and the guidance of wise mentors. Inviting a mature believer with the same gift to come alongside you to help you is a good way to grow up into your gifting. In addition, it is wise to allow God to present you with opportunities to use your gifts rather than going out on your own to find opportunities.

Take the apostle Paul for instance. He was a very gifted man. But did you know that he spent about 14 years learning and seeking the Lord after his conversion experience? What was he doing? He was in part maturing in his giftings. It was important for him to take this time to mature so that he would be properly equipped to accomplish the work that God had planned for him.

Understanding that the Holy Spirit has given you specific gifts to serve the Body of Christ is part of your true identity. Your spiritual gifts are part of who you are in Christ and Who Christ is in you.

Walking in your true identity involves using the gifts you know the Holy Spirit has given you by serving others. We often say that nothing God gives you is for your own consumption, but always for blessing and benefiting others. And so the gifts of the Spirit are the part of your true identity that should be practically applied in the community of believers.

NOTE - It is helpful to understand that not every church or denomination views spiritual gifts in the same way. Your church for example, may not recognize certain gifts like the gift of prophecy, word of knowledge, tongues and interpretation of tongues. If you have questions about spiritual gifts, ask your church leaders for direction.

The one thing we do not want to do is bring division into the body of Christ over differences of interpretation of Scripture. Respect for authority and consideration for each person will go far in bringing unity and acceptance, and the proper use of our spiritual gifts. The apostle Paul submitted himself to the authority of the church leaders in Jerusalem. (Acts 15). He did not presume that simply because he was an apostle, he could make decisions affecting the church apart from those who were its leaders. So he sought their advice and counsel. And he also relied on the wisdom and direction of God in those times when he disagreed with the leaders in the church. (See **Galatians 2**)

✝ REFLECTION QUESTIONS

1. Read **Matthew 25:14-30**. How do you think this parable relates to spiritual gifts?

Who do the people in this story represent in the Kingdom of God?

What did the faithful servants do?

What does the wicked servant do?

What is the outcome for each one?

2. Jesus is the only person who has walked the earth who had all the spiritual gifts mentioned in Scripture. He said that His disciples would do the same and even greater things than He did. (See **John 14:12**). What do you think Jesus means when He says even greater things than these?

   Have you seen examples of this? Why or why not, do you think?

3. Take a spiritual gifts inventory to assess your gifts. There are several available Online.

   Do you see any way you have been using your gifts possibly even without being aware that you had these gifts?

4. If you have a gift and you are not sure what it means or how it is used, begin a search and study mission to learn more about this gift. Start with Scripture references to your gift. You may want to use commentaries, Bible dictionaries, etc. to learn more. You can also ask mature believers and church leaders for their perspective.

👥💬 GROUP DISCUSSION QUESTIONS

1. Read **1 Corinthians 12:4-7** (TPT):

   verse 4 - *"It is the same Holy Spirit who continues to distribute many different varieties of gifts."*

   verse 5 - *"The Lord Yahweh is one, and he is the one who apportions to believers different varieties of ministries."* (See Ephesians 4:7-16)

   verse 6 - *"The same God distributes different kinds of miracles that accomplish different results through each believer's gift and ministry as he energizes and activates them."*

   verse 7 - *"Each believer is given continuous revelation by the Holy Spirit to benefit not just himself but all."*

   Describe the role of Holy Spirit, Jesus and God the Father in spiritual gifts. Why do you think they each have a specific, defined role?

2. In **2 Corinthians 3:17** we read, *"Now the Lord is the Spirit, and where the Spirit of the Lord is, there is freedom."*

"[Our] freedom is a reality to be appropriated, not a possibility to which [we] must be gradually introduced."   Robert Banks, pastor

Based on the Scripture, what do you think Banks is telling us?

How does this relate to what we have learned about The Holy Spirit and spiritual gifts?

3. What spiritual gifts have you seen in operation? Were the core principles followed?

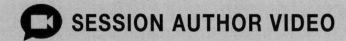

SESSION AUTHOR VIDEO

Watch the SESSION 6 - *SPIRITUAL GIFTS* author video

TrueIdentityStudy.com/walking-ti-videos-audio

DEBBIE JONES
Debbie gives an overview of Session 6 - *Spiritual Gifts,* along with a personal example.

🚶 WALKING IT HOME

APPLYING WHAT YOU HAVE LEARNED

Divide into groups of two or three.

Share with each other about your spiritual gifts and the direction you believe God is giving you for the use of your gifts. If you know what your gifts are and have experienced using them, share an example.

 **PRAYING IT FORWARD**

Stay in your small groups.

Read **Acts 13:1-3** and then pray for God to create the opportunity for each person to use their spiritual gifts.

_____

_____

_____

_____

_____

_____

_____

_____

_____

_____

_____

_____

_____

_____

_____

_____

_____

_____

_____

_____

_____

_____

_____

_____

📖 RESOURCES - FOR FURTHER STUDY

RECOMMENDED BOOKS
Discover Your God-Given Gifts - *by Don and Katie Fortune*
Experiencing God - *by Henry Blackaby*

KEY SCRIPTURES MENTIONING SPIRITUAL GIFTS

1 Peter 4:10-12
"As each has received a gift, use it to serve one another, as good stewards of God's varied grace: whoever speaks, as one who speaks oracles of God; whoever serves, as one who serves by the strength that God supplies—in order that in everything God may be glorified through Jesus Christ. To him belong glory and dominion forever and ever. Amen."

1 Corinthians 12:7-10 - **Nine gifts mentioned** (Also see **12:28-30**)
"To each is given the manifestation of the Spirit for the common good. For to one is given through the Spirit the utterance of wisdom, and to another the utterance of knowledge according to the same Spirit, to another faith by the same Spirit, to another gifts of healing by the one Spirit, to another the working of miracles, to another prophecy, to another the ability to distinguish between spirits, to another various kinds of tongues, to another the interpretation of tongues."

Ephesians 4:11-12 - **Five gifts mentioned**
"And he gave the apostles, the prophets, the evangelists, the shepherds and teachers, to equip the saints for the work of ministry, for building up the body of Christ."

Romans 12:6-8 - **Seven gifts mentioned**
"Having gifts that differ according to the grace given to us, let us use them: if prophecy, in proportion to our faith; if service, in our serving; the one who teaches, in his teaching; the one who exhorts, in his exhortation; the one who contributes, in generosity; the one who leads, with zeal; the one who does acts of mercy, with cheerfulness."

NOTES

Session 7

Crossing the Jordan

JENNIFER BROMMET

"And when the soles of the feet of the priests bearing the ark of the Lord, the Lord of all the earth, shall rest in the waters of the Jordan, the waters of the Jordan shall be cut off from flowing, and the waters coming down from above shall stand in one heap."
Joshua 3:13

Walking in your true identity is a faith journey with many challenging valleys and mountaintops! For God's people, spiritual preparation is a vital element in your faith journey and being able to truly walk and live freely in your true identity. For it is being in a right relationship with God that brings the supernatural power of God into your life, ministry and work.

SELF STUDY

NOTE: Be sure to complete the Self Study, Core Principles, and Reflection Questions BEFORE you meet with your group each session.

We need a lot of encouragement along this faith journey. Thankfully, God has given us all we need to walk it in victory and freedom through the power of the Holy Spirit within us, His Word, and a multitude of examples of His faithfulness and love for us. One prime example is the story of Joshua leading the Israelites across the Jordan River into the Promised Land and God's unfailing faithfulness. (**Joshua 3 & 4**)

First, let's look at some history to understand why this is such a big deal. Many years prior, Moses had sent out 12 spies (1 from each of the 12 tribes of Israel, including Joshua and Caleb) to "spy out the Promised Land" that God had promised the nation of Israel *(see map)*. They came back with a report of it being *"a land flowing with milk and honey"* and showed them the fruit of the land, but *"the people who dwell there were strong, and the cities were fortified and very large. The land that devours its inhabitants, and all the people that we saw in it are of great height. We seemed like grasshoppers next to them."* (**Numbers 13:27-29; 31-33**)

It lists all the terrifying, giant "ites"- Amalekites, Hittites, Jebusites, Amorites, Canaanites, who dwelled in the Promised Land. The Israelites were petrified of these people and begged Moses to take them back to Egypt!

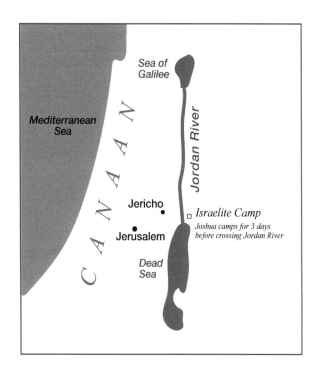

Sea of Galilee

Mediterranean Sea

Jordan River

CANAAN

Jericho

Jerusalem

Dead Sea

☐ *Israelite Camp*
Joshua camps for 3 days before crossing Jordan River

However, Caleb and Joshua were the only two of the twelve spies who gave a positive report, believing that God would give them victory and fulfill His promise for the land. Due to their faith and trust in God, they were the only ones of the Israelites at that time who would see and inherit the Promised Land (see **Numbers 14:6-30**).

Fast forward 40 years. Moses is dead and Joshua is Israel's new leader (now about 80 years old). The Israelites have wandered around the desert for 40 years, and now Joshua is tasked to lead the people (about 2 million) across the Jordan into the Promised Land. Joshua and the nation of Israel have come to the banks of the Jordan River, which is now at flood stage (harvest time), deeper than normal and with a stronger than usual current; and remember, has all those terrifying "ites" on the other side!

Continue your self study with the Core Principles below. Pray and ask the Lord to reveal any new insights, understanding or personal application. Look up all Scripture verses to become more familiar with where they are in your Bible, and make notes.

⌐ CORE PRINCIPLES

1. At the River
(Read **Joshua 3:1-6**)

Before the Israelites were to cross over the Jordan River, Joshua instructed the people to camp by the river to prepare and *"Consecrate yourselves, for tomorrow the Lord will do wonders among you."* (v5) Consecrate means to set apart, prepare, dedicate. There needed to be a spiritual preparation for them before the events of the next day.

They knew there were a lot of obstacles waiting for them on the other side but even crossing the Jordan was a miracle in itself. Why? Because they were crossing it at its annual flood stage, which for most would mean certain death. This was going to take a "Parting of the Red Sea" type miracle, which was why it took immense faith and resolve for Joshua, the priests, and the Israelites to trust God would do as He promised.

Spiritual preparation in waiting and obedience is part of our true identity as God's sons and daughters. Waiting is productive, not just killing time, but then we must take action. Faith is not passive.

God is Working Upstream
(Read **Joshua 3:7-10; 16**)

God had gone before the Israelites to prepare for the time when they were to cross the Jordan River. There was no bridge or ferry for them to use, they had to go in it and through it! Impossible? Yes! But God knew the perfect timing to stop the flow of the river upstream in Adam (about 16 miles north) so that when the Priests stepped into the river, the water would stop and "stand in one heap" (v 13). Think about the logistics of that!

Take comfort in knowing that God is working "out of sight – upstream" to prepare you for crossing your "Jordan River" and what lies on the other side. He is removing obstacles, orchestrating events and circumstances for you to step into His purpose and plan for you. And although it can be difficult to wait and trust in things you can't see, as you grow in your intimacy with God, you can trust God in His call and how He is speaking to you.

I have a little plaque on my desk reminding me that, *"A trusting heart walks through life with a faithful God. Trust in the Lord with all your heart."* **Proverbs 3:5**

Isaiah 57:14 - *"And it shall be said, 'Build up, build up, prepare the way, remove every obstruction from my people's way.'"*

Exodus 23:20 - *"See, I am sending an angel ahead of you to guard you along the way and to bring you to the place I have prepared."*

Ephesians 2:10 - *"For we are his workmanship, created in Christ Jesus for good works, which God prepared beforehand, that we should walk in them."*

Stepping Into the Jordan
(Read **Joshua 3:11-15**)

Once the Israelites were ready, the priests carried the Ark of the Covenant, and since it was the ark that represented God's person and power, they alone were to take the ark to the edge of the water, be the first to step into the raging water, and stand still in it.

Side note: The Ark of the Covenant represented the person and promises of God. It pointed to the fact that as the people of Israel set out to cross the Jordan, invade, and possess the land, they must do so not in their own strength, but in God's for it was God Himself who was going before them as their source of victory.

It was not until "the soles of the feet of the priests bearing the ark were dipped in the brink of the water" that the water stopped flowing (from 16 miles upstream) and piled up in a heap so the people of Israel could cross. They didn't stand there and wait for God to stop the flow of water first. They had to TAKE THE FIRST STEP! Wow! It took enormous faith for them to do this! Remember: flood stage, deep, fast current, certain death.

What do we gather from this? It reminds us of our part in the plan of God. After productive waiting and preparation, we must learn to step out in faith and obedience to the principles and promises of Scripture and the things God is calling us to be and do.

Fear can be an immense barrier to stepping in the river. Fear of the unknown. Fear of letting go of bad habits/strongholds. Fear that nothing will change and it will just be like it was before. Fear that it will be too difficult and you will fail. Fear of rejection, hurt or disappointment. Fear of what awaits on the other side.

Have faith to step into the river knowing fully that God has you and will give you everything you need to cross (**Romans 8:31-39**). Faith implies action, and oftentimes we have to take the step of faith before God shows His power or answer. Remember, you have the Holy Spirit living in you and empowering you! You know full well that you are a redeemed, sanctified, child of God and you have rock-solid security in knowing your true identity in Christ! He has gone before you to prepare the way to cross whatever "Jordan River" you are facing. You can trust God 100% and rest in His promises. Go ahead, put your foot in the water!

1 Thessalonians 5:24 - *"He who calls you is faithful; he will surely do it!"*

Psalm 86:11 (NIV) - *"Teach me your way, Lord, that I may rely on your faithfulness; give me an undivided heart, that I may fear your name."*

Psalm 25:3 (TLB) - *"None of those who have faith in God will ever be disgraced for trusting him."*

4. Crossing the River
(Read **Joshua 3: 16-17; 4:10-19**)

The miracle happened! The priests with the ark stepped into the river and the flow of water stopped and piled up into a heap! They then "stood firmly on dry ground in the midst of the Jordan, and all Israel was passing over on dry ground until all the nation (remember we're talking 2 million people here – this took a while) finished passing over the Jordan." (v17) The visual of this blows my mind!

The awesome thing is, God is still in the miracle business! They may not feel as spectacular as parting the sea or stopping up a torrential river, but every time you "step" into a "Jordan" and cross, you are demonstrating incredible faith and trust, and will experience God doing a miraculous and monumental thing in your life.

Here are some "tools" God has given you to help you cross the river:

- Understanding your personality, spiritual gifts, and how you best grow closer to God, serve Him, and give Him glory in who He made you to be.

- Be reminded of what you are saved from and saved for (See Session 1 and 2). Have a grateful heart.

- Keep close to the Lord as a best friend. Spend time with Him. Abide in Him and walk intimately with Him daily.

- Hear God speak to you through His Word, as well as be "tuned in" and hear God speaking to you in other ways than through His Word.

- You are not crossing the "river" alone. You are Holy Spirit empowered!

- Step out in faith, cross the river, and trust God fully to help you do all He has called and purposed for you to be and to do.

Philippians 4:13 (TLB) -*"For I can do everything God asks me to with the help of Christ who gives me the strength and power."*

Romans 8:31 - *"What then shall we say to these things? If God is for us, who can be against us?"*

5. In Remembrance
(Read **Joshua 4**)

Why do you feel it is important to remember what God has done in your life? I call it, "looking in the rear-view mirror." When faced with a new faith challenge, it is helpful to look back and remember how God provided, gave wisdom and protection, and brought you through, so that you are reminded that He is not going to abandon you or forsake you now. It is also faith-building and God-glorifying for others to hear what God has done in your life. The Israelites felt the same way!

Hebrews 13:5 - *"I will never leave you nor forsake you."*

The Israelites built an altar out of stones from the Jordan in remembrance of what God had done and as a testimony of His faithfulness. Twelve men —one from each tribe — were instructed to take a stone from the bottom of the Jordan and carry it to the bank of the river. Note in verse 4 that these were LARGE stones that the men were told to "take up on your shoulder!"

They wanted to build a memorial with these stones as a reminder of the miraculous thing God had done. It would leave a visual to strike up a conversation about a pile of stones and give testimony of God's faithfulness to future generations.

"Large stones taken from the bottom of the Jordan river?" one will ask. "How is that possible?"

"Well, let me tell you how it happened . . .!"

Joshua 4:4-7 (TLB) - *"So Joshua summoned the twelve men and told them, "Go out into the middle of the Jordan where the Ark is. Each of you is to carry out a stone on your shoulder—twelve stones in all, one for each of the twelve tribes. We will use them to build a monument so that in the future, when your children ask, 'What is this monument for?' you can tell them, 'It is to remind us that the Jordan River stopped flowing when the Ark of God went across!' The monument will be a permanent reminder to the people of Israel of this amazing miracle."*

1 Chronicles 16:9 (TLB) - *"Sing to him; yes, sing his praises And tell of his marvelous works."*

6. **Persevering in Your True Identity & Walking Free in the Promised Land**
(Read **Joshua 5 & 6**)

Once the Israelites crossed the Jordan, they were not home free. They could not just waltz into Jericho and announce they were now claiming their "Promised Land" and were in charge. They had to look to God for direction, wisdom and strength in facing all those "ites" and winning a battle for Jericho and the Promised Land. God performed another miracle in the victory over Jericho, again proving His power and faithfulness.

Once we cross over our "Jordan River" and pursue God's call and promises in our lives, things may not get easier. In fact, they may be even more challenging. It often takes perseverance to maintain intimacy with God and walk freely in our true identity. Remember from the *True Identity Study* when we talked about facing a relentless enemy? He (satan) will continue to assault you with lies and deception and do all he can to keep you from an intimate relationship with God.

HOWEVER, be encouraged in all that God has deposited in your through this study and that you have been given EVERYTHING you need to walk in freedom and victory in your true identity in Christ. You are a child of the one true King! God wants nothing more than for you to come into a right relationship with Him and live a joyful and abundant life, free from lies, fear, anxiety, pride, strongholds and bondages. He wants you to be healed and empowered to pursue all that He designed you to be!

Wait productively and prepare for God's next step, and when the time is right, step out in faith, cross your Jordan with confidence, and walk free in all God designed you to be!

Proverbs 3:1-8 - *"My son, do not forget my teaching, but let your heart keep my commandments, for length of days and years of life and peace they will add to you. Let not steadfast love and faithfulness forsake you; bind them around your neck; write them on the tablet of your heart. So you will find favor and good success in the sight of God and man.*

Trust in the Lord with all your heart, and do not lean on your own understanding. In all your ways acknowledge him, and he will make straight your paths. Be not wise in your own eyes; fear the Lord, and turn away from evil. It will be healing to your flesh and refreshment to your bones."

Psalm 32:8 - *"I will instruct you and teach you in the way you should go; I will counsel you with my eye on you."*

103

✝ REFLECTION QUESTIONS

1. Joshua instructed the Israelites to "sanctify" themselves and prepare for the things God was going to do the next day. Are you in a right, intimate relationship with God and seeking His will and empowerment in your life? Are you in any sin?

   How do you need to "consecrate" yourself to prepare for what God has next for you in your life?

2. Are you taking comfort in knowing that God is working upstream to prepare you for crossing your "river" and what lies on the other side?

   Do you believe He is going before you to remove obstacles, orchestrating events and circumstances for you to step into His purpose and plan for you? If not, why?

3. What is Your Jordan River right now?

   What is standing in the way of you trusting God and stepping into the river?
   Ask God to show you what it is that is holding you back from fully surrendering and trusting in Him, and to give you the faith to "step into the river".

4. Are you in the middle of "crossing a river"? What challenges are you facing in crossing?

   Ask God what it is He is desiring to transform in you through this process. What steps can you take to persevere and make it to the other side?

5. Read **1 Thessalonians 5:24**
    How have you witnessed God's provision and empowerment firsthand in your life?

    What is a visual reminder of God's faithfulness in your life and "memorial stones" you can use to tell others or your children about God's faithfulness? Give testimony to God's faithfulness in your life!

6. What type of things can keep you from maintaining an intimate relationship with God and abiding in Him daily?

    Having completed this study, do you have a deeper understanding of steps you can take to walk freely in your true identity each and every day? If so, what are they? Pray and ask the Lord to help you develop the habit of spending time with him daily and trusting and abiding in Him, no matter what "Jordan Rivers" you may face.

Prayer:
"Dear Heavenly Father, help me to fully trust you as I am facing "Jordan Rivers" in my life. Help me to put my hand in yours and take the first step knowing full well You have gone before me and prepared the way in which I am to walk. Give me bold faith and obedience in trusting You will give me all I need to walk in victory and joy in all You have designed me to be. I give You the honor, glory and praise for all the amazing things you have done in my life! In Jesus' Name~ Amen."

👥💬 GROUP DISCUSSION QUESTIONS

2 Corinthians 5:17 - *"Therefore, if anyone is in Christ, he is a new creation. The old has passed away; behold the new has come."*

1. Why do you think it was important for the Israelites to sanctify themselves and prepare for what God was going to do the next day?

    Why are spiritual preparation and productive waiting vital elements in your faith walk?

2. Why do you think God brings us to seemingly impossible situations (Jordan Rivers) in our lives?

    What type of things keep us from fully trusting God and taking the first step into the river?

3. Why do you think God allows "Jordan River" experiences in our lives *before* bringing us into the promise on the other side?

    How can you glorify God in trusting Him to cross the river and walk freely in His promises on the other side?

4. Why is it important to remember the things God has done in our lives and share them with others?

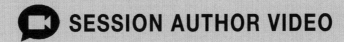

SESSION AUTHOR VIDEO

Watch the SESSION 7 - *CROSSING THE JORDAN* author video

<u>TrueIdentityStudy.com/walking-ti-videos-audio</u>

JENNIFER BROMMET

Jennifer gives an overview of Session 7 - *Crossing the Jordan,* a personal example and brief study wrap-up.

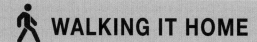

WALKING IT HOME

APPLYING WHAT YOU HAVE LEARNED

Divide into groups of 2 or 3.

Share with one another a "Jordan River" experience in your life. How did God, or is God, working in extraordinary ways in it?

How can you give testimony to what God has done?

PRAYING IT FORWARD

Pray for one another for whatever stage you may in with your personal "Jordan River." Ask the Lord to empower each of you as you trust Him in each step of "walking in your true identity" and how you can then best give testimony to God's faithfulness in your lives.

📖 RESOURCES - FOR FURTHER STUDY

RECOMMENDED BOOKS
Abiding in Christ - *by Andrew Murray*
Abide in Jesus - *by Helmut Haubeil* (PDF)
Be Anxious for Nothing - *by Max Lucado*
Living Free in Christ - *by Neil Anderson*
Shaken: Discovering Your True Identity in the Midst of Life's Storms - *by Tim Tebow*
The Ruthless Elimination of Hurry - *by John Mark Comer*
True Identity - *by Jennifer Brommet*

Devotionals
One Year Book of Psalms – *by William Petersen and Randy Petersen*
Our Daily Bread 2021 Devotional – *by Our Daily Bread Ministries*
The Chosen: 40 Days with Jesus (Book 1 & 2) – *by Amanda Jenkins, Kristen Hendricks and Dallas Jenkins*

Christian Fiction - (see list on Page 45)

January 2014
Blog Post- Jennifer Brommet

TAKE THE FIRST STEP

Each New Year I pray and ask God to give me a "Banner" Bible verse or verses for the year. I have been doing this for about 6 years now and continue to be amazed at how right on, encouraging, and supportive they always are. I really shouldn't be, since His Word is LIVING and active in me and from the One who knows and loves me best!

So as I was praying at the end of 2013 for God to give me this year's verse(s), I woke up on January 1, in my daughter's flat in London, with the verse, Joshua 3:10 clearly in my mind. It wasn't a verse I was already familiar with so I looked it up.

"And Joshua said, here is how you will know the living God is among you and that he will without fail drive out from before you the Canaanites, the Hittites, the Hivites, the Perizzites, the Girgashites, the Amorites, and the Jebusites."

My first thought was, *"That's a lot of "ites"* and what in the world does this mean for me? Certainly THIS can't be my year banner verse?"

The Lord then encouraged me to also read verse 13.

"And when the soles of the feet of the priest bearing the ark of the Lord, the Lord of all the earth, shall rest in the waters of the Jordan, the waters of the Jordan shall be cut off from flowing, and the waters coming down from above shall stand in one heap."

Okay, now I was really confused. I prayed and asked the Lord to show me what this meant for me, and were these indeed my year "banner" verses?

He spoke into my spirit and told me that He was going to remove any obstacles (the "ites") from my life this next year that would hinder me from doing what He calls me to do, BUT, and there's always that "but", I had to TAKE THE FIRST STEP, as the priests did when crossing the Jordan with the Ark of the Covenant. I knew that this was a very significant Biblical event, but still not understanding what it had to do with me.

As I looked further, (read all of Joshua Chapter 3 for details surrounding this event), I was reminded that the Israelites, after wandering the desert for many years, needed to cross the Jordan River to enter the Promised land on the other side. They knew there were a lot of obstacles waiting for them on the other side (i.e. all those "ites"), but even crossing the Jordan was a miracle in itself. Why? Because they were crossing it at its annual flood stage, which for most would mean certain death. This was going to take a "Parting of the Red Sea" type miracle, which was why it took great faith for Joshua, the priests, and the Israelites to trust God would do as He promised. And, as a side note, it was not until the "soles of the feet of the priests" rested in the water that the Lord would stop the rivers from flowing. They had to TAKE THE FIRST STEP!

God showed me that He was doing His part "up-stream" to prepare the perfect timing, connections, circumstances, and miraculous intervention He has for my life, just as He did for the Israelites in stopping the flow of the river so they could cross. But, like the priests, I have to do my part in TAKING THE FIRST STEP. I would imagine as those priests stood at the banks of the raging Jordan River they were terrified at the thought of stepping into the river not knowing if they would be swept away to their deaths or indeed witness another miracle. But they had solid faith in God, that even though they did not know what would happen next, they could trust the One who was leading them. How many times have I stood at a "Jordan River" in my life, terrified of what I was facing and uncertain of what would happen if I stepped in the river, and what lay on the other side? Many times!

It all came together then. I knew that indeed these were my "banner verses" for this New Year. God assured me that for all the times I will be standing at the banks of my "Jordan Rivers" this year, I can trust Him to safely carry me through and across, and, into what lies on the other side. That when I have no clue what lies around the bend or what may be the final outcome of a challenging situation, which is most of the time, He is always working "upstream" on my behalf. He is continuing to go before me and prepare the way in which I will go, but I have to keep TAKING THOSE FIRST STEPS and He will be right there to take my hand and lovingly lead me each step thereafter. I can rest in knowing the ONE who is leading me.

I praise God for His faithfulness and love for me! For His perfect plan for my life and helping me to continue to trust Him as I step into my "Jordan Rivers" to the promises and purposes He has for my life.

Looking forward to another adventurous year crossing the "Jordan's!"

Jennifer Brommet

Post note: 2014 DID turn out to be quite an adventurous and challenging year! The Lord helped me cross several "Jordan Rivers" that year, and many more since, but I can attest to His amazing faithfulness, growing me in my faith, and allowing me to draw even closer in my relationship with Him, and continuing to set me free to be all He created me to be!

What is your "Jordan River" right now? Pray and ask the Lord to help you trust Him and take the first step to cross it. Other encouraging verses you may like to read: **Exodus 23:30**, **Psalm 85:13**, and **Isaiah 57:14**.

REMEMBER WHO YOU ARE!

Therefore, if anyone is in Christ, he is a new creation... 2 Corinthians 5:17

In the Mirror of God's Word, I See...

1 Samuel 12:22	I am His own.
1 Samuel 16:7	He sees my heart.
2 Kings 20:5	He heals me.
1 Chron. 28:8	I will pass on an inheritance.
Job 23:10	He knows the way that I take.
Psalm 16:11	He gives me eternal pleasures at His right hand.
Psalm 21:6	He makes me glad with the joy of His presence.
Psalm 27:4	I will gaze upon the beauty of the Lord forever.
Psalm 27:10	He will never forsake me.
Psalm 34:18	He is near me.
Psalm 45:11	He is enthralled by my beauty.
Psalm 91:14	He rescues me.
Psalm 103:4	He crowns me with love and compassion.
Psalm 107:9	He satisfies my hunger with good things.
Psalm 139:14	I am wonderfully made.
Proverbs 12:25	He cheers my heart.
Proverbs 15:4	I speak words of life to others.
Isaiah 41:18	He makes my wilderness like Eden.
Isaiah 53:4	He bears my pain.
Isaiah 61:3	He gives me a crown of beauty instead of ashes.
Isaiah 61:10	He wraps me in a robe of righteousness.
Isaiah 62:2	He calls me by a new name.
Isaiah 64:8	I am His workmanship.
Jeremiah 1:5	He knows me.
Jeremiah 14:9	I bear His name.
Jeremiah 31:3	He loves me with an everlasting love.
Mark 6:31	He takes me to a quiet place and gives me rest.
John 7:24	He does not judge me by appearances.
John 8:36	He sets me free.
Romans 15:7	I am accepted in the Beloved.
2 Cor. 3:16	He sees me as I am.
2 Cor. 4:17	He turns my hardship to glory.
Galatians 5:1	He delivers me.
Ephesians 1:3	He blesses me with every spiritual blessing.
Philippians 3:13	He redeems my past.
2 Thes. 2:16	He gives me hope.
2 Peter 1:3	He gives me everything I need.

NOTES

Study Wrap-up

JENNIFER BROMMET

"Beloved, I pray that all may go well with you and that you may be in good health, as it goes well with your soul. For I rejoiced greatly when the brothers came and testified to your truth, as indeed you are walking in the truth."
3 John 1:2-3

 Watch the WALK ON! video
TrueIdentityStudy.com/walking-ti-videos-audio

You have come to the end of the *Walking in Your True Identity Study*!
It is our hope that your journey deepened your understanding of your salvation, intimacy with God, hearing from God, the person and work of the Holy Spirit in you, and how your true identity plays into crossing your "Jordan" and walking in freedom in all God designed you to be.

So, what's next? Your true identity walk continues in your *everyday life* by putting into action all God has deposited in you through this study and developing godly habits of abiding in Christ by:

• **Confronting lies** that present themselves to you and replacing them with Scriptural truths.

• **Making room** in your life for intimacy with God, and hearing from God. Be in the Word.

• **Daily worship and delight in God**, and gratitude for knowing you and saving you.

• **Yielding to the Holy Spirit's work in your life** – forming Christ in you, revealing Christ to you, bearing fruit in you and giving you the spiritual gifts with which to play your part in building up the Body of Christ.

• **Productively waiting for God to complete His work upstream** whenever you face obstacles and uncertainties.

• **Trusting God to "take the first step"** and in each step of your faith walk.

• **Believe God has gone before you** to prepare the way and will give you all you need to continue to be healed and set-free to walk and live in all He created you to be.

Here are some additional ways to help you continue walking in your true identity:

1. **Look back** through the *True Identity Study* and the notes you took.

2. **Re-read** *Walking in Your True Identity*. Reading the two right after each other helps you form a complete and clear picture of your true identity and how to walk in it every day.

3. **Order your daily and weekly rhythm** around seeking time alone with God: to become intimate with Him, to listen to Him, and to grow in your knowledge of His Word.

4. **Maintain a journal** as you receive impressions and insights from Him. Writing them down helps you remember them, opens the way for more insights, and gives you a reference in case you do forget.

5. **Walk the walk!** It has been said that the best way to know God is to obey Him. The Holy Spirit has given you gifts, and partners with you in prayer, so you can contribute to the kingdom work.
   - Discuss avenues for the use of your gifts in your church or faith community
   - Ask the Lord to give you a Kingdom Assignment: a particular area of ministry to support, pray for and get involved in

6. **Be quick to recognize, renounce and replace lies with truth.** Satan will not stop barraging you with lies, from subtle deceptions to blatant whoppers, about yourself, about God, and about others. Reaffirm daily who you are in Christ and Who Christ is in you as part of your devotions. If necessary, write out which part of your true identity comes under attack the most and put it in a prominent place as a daily reminder. Continue to WALK ON in God's TRUTH!

WALKING IN YOUR TRUE IDENTITY STUDY SUMMARY

✓ Remember what you have been saved *from.*

✓ Rejoice in what you have been saved *for.*

✓ Meet with God daily, deepen your intimacy with Him, and *abide* in Him.

✓ Learn to listen and hear God clearly.

✓ Allow the Holy Spirit to have ALL of you.

✓ Trust God to do all He has purposed for you through the Holy Spirit in you.

✓ Engage in your spiritual gifting, so as to lift up the body of Christ.

✓ Look at your "Jordan River" experience as an opportunity to trust God at a deeper level and grow in your faith walk. Cross over to your "Promised Land"!

✓ Step out in faith in what God is telling and leading you to do. **1 Thessalonians 5:24**)

✓ Put on the whole armor of God each day (**Ephesians 6:10-20**). Keep deflecting lies and replacing them with God's truth.

✓ Take authority over the enemy, use the keys Jesus gave us. (**Matthew 16:19, Luke 10:19**)

✓ Persevere in JOY! (**James 1:2-4**) and WALK ON! (**3 John 1:4**)

📖 RESOURCES - FOR FURTHER STUDY

WORD STUDY
Word studies are a great way to dig deeper in the Word and broaden your understanding of Biblical principles and life application. Below are some suggestions to get you started.

Using a **Concordance** (check if you have one in the back of your Bible) or use an Online Bible Concordance and look up the following words and the scriptures listed for each:

Abide/Abides	Fruit	Meditate	Securely
Always	Gift/Gifts	Mind	Spirit
Awesome	Grow	Near	Strength
Believe	Hears	Nothing	Teach
Bless/Blessed	Help	Path/Paths	Thanks
Called	Hope/Hopes	Peace	Transformed
Confidence	Joy/Joyful	Power	Trust/Trusts
Devotion	Kind/Kindness	Praise	Truth
Dwells	Knows	Pray	Understand
Eternal	Led	Promised	Wait
Faith/Faithful/Faithfulness	Listen/Listens	Renew	Walk
Forgive	Lives	Rooted	Will
Free	Loved	Savior	Word

True Identity Ministries has additional resources available to help you deepen your spiritual life and strengthen your devotional habits:

Fellowship with the Father Prayer Guide
A free 30-day prayer guide PDF by Remco Brommet based on the weekly *True Identity Prayer Digests* that have guided us in prayer through the turbulence of the year 2020. For more information and to download: https://www.TrueIdentityMinistries.org/ministries

The Deeper Life Blog - Subscribe to Remco's Blog - - https://deeperlifeblog.com/
This blog aims to enthrall you with the amazing delight of a daily, personal walk with God, and to help you listen to Him, while alerting you to the sense of urgency that these turbulent times add to our faith walk. You'll find articles and short videos. Subscribe to be alerted to new content. You'll find it both informative and inspiring!

The Abundant Life Podcast - Remco Brommet
Exploring the deeper aspects of walking with God along with insights in prayer and abiding in Christ. Available on *Spotify*.

Check in with our **True Identity Ministries website** https://www.TrueIdentityMinistries.org/ and the **True Identity Study website** https://TrueIdentityStudy.com/ for updates and new resources available to help you understand, walk and live in freedom in your TRUE identity!

Please be sure to **Email us** at info@trueidentityministries.org with questions, feedback and stories of how the *Walking In Your True Identity Study* has impacted you and your group!

NOTES

Thank you for leading a small group through the *Walking in Your True Identity Study*! May you experience a deepening walk with the Lord through it. As a small group leader, you manage the behind-the-scenes details and help set a positive and loving group environment by encouraging participants to share their ideas, understanding and experiences, as you grow together.

Here are some pointers to help you lead a small group through the *Walking in Your True Identity Study*.

- Your role as small group leader is to serve your group, and help shepherd them through the study. Pray the Lord will give you HIS love for your group exhibited through your actions and words. Your goal is to help create a loving, accepting, "safe" environment for your group to feel they can share and be real, and trust what they share will be kept in confidence.

- God will use your personality, gifting and experiences to perfectly encourage and minister to the members of your group.

- Set some group "ground rules" at the beginning:
    * No cell phones or electronic devices during study time, or phones on silent.
    * Remind them to refrain from discussing politics, church denominations, books or movies. The focus of the study is to be on the Lord and things that unify.

- Remind them that everything shared in the group is confidential, and is not to be shared outside the group.

- Everyone is there to learn, and there are always new things to learn. We are not there to judge one another, but to encourage one another and build each other up.

- When discussion gets off track, gently and with humor, rein things back in and refocus the discussion.

- Set the example or help get discussions started if needed by briefly sharing from your own experience. Encourage each participant to share if they desire, but don't be afraid of silence at times. Privately encourage "dominating" participants to help others share by waiting before they speak.

- Small group leaders are not counselors. Your role as a group leader is to listen, love and pray for your study group, and direct them to Jesus and God's Word for answers. Please guard against the desire to "preach" or teach group members what to do in any particular situation. Show them scripture that may help them and offer to pray with them. The aim is to help group members go to God's Word, His truth, and seek God personally for Him to speak specifically into their situation.

Key Aspects of a Small Group Leader

- Establishes and maintains an atmosphere of unity and cooperation within the group.
- Prepares for each session and keeps the focus of each session clearly in mind.
- Encourages each participant to share in the discussion process and group activities.
- Remains neutral in most cases to help participants work out their own solutions with the Lord.
- Integrates participants' expertise or experience into the discussion.
- Reduces and contains distractions.

Your overall aim is to help build group unity, bonding, offer encouragement, care for your group, and point them to Jesus. The Lord is the one who does the powerful transformation in our lives. Help set the stage for participants to be in a place where they can connect with and hear from God throughout the study experience.

Study Preparation

As a group leader it is good to be prepared ahead of time for each study session. Do the *Self-Study, Core Principles* and *Reflection Questions*. The main emphasis in this study is to help participants learn how to do self-study, become more familiar with the Word, and go to God in prayer for answers and personal application. Review and answer the *Group Discussion Questions* to know content, watch the *Session Author video*, and plan how you would like to shepherd your group through each session. Since the bulk of this study is done individually *before* you meet as a group, you will have a bit more time for discussion and review, but still need to keep an eye on your time. The more familiar you are with the session topic, material, and timing for each segment, the more you can help keep your group focused and on track.

Suggested Timing for a 90 Minute Study Session:

*Have the video(s) queued and ready to go before starting. Always start on time.

Welcome - group arrives and gets settled	5 minutes
Review the session *Self-Study, Core Principles* & *Reflection Questions*	10 minutes
Group Discussion	35-40 minutes
Watch the *Session Author video*	10 minutes
Walking it Home - Applying What you Have Learned	10-15 minutes
Prayer (Praying it Forward)	10 minutes
Group Leader closes the session with a brief prayer	

Video Setup

* Plan in advance how you are going to show the videos. Access the videos through this link **TrueIdentityStudy.com/walking-ti-videos-audio**
Connecting to the video/audio files will depend on your equipment and set-up.

Optional Activity: Decide as a group if you would like to have an additional meeting after the last session. Have a meal together and share what God did in your lives throughout the study. Have time to pray together and share communion together.

Self-Study Helps

Kay Arthur, *The New How to Study Your Bible: Discover the Life-Changing Approach to God's Word* (Eugene, OR: Harvest House Publishers, 1994/2010) p. 9.

Session 2: Saved For

John Piper, *Desiring God* (Sisters, OR: Multnomah, 2003), p. 17-18.

John Piper, Sermons at www.desiringgod.org, October 13, 2012.

John Piper, *God is the Gospel: Meditations on God's Love as the Gift of Himself* (Wheaton, IL: Crossway Books, 2011)

John Mark Comer, *The Ruthless Elimination of Hurry* (Colorado Springs, CO: Waterbrook, 2019) p. 21-22

Session 4: Hearing From God

For a fuller study on how to hear God's voice see Mark and Patti Virkler, *4 Keys to Hearing God's Voice* (Shippensburg, PA: Destiny Image ® Publishers, Inc., 2010).

Session 5: The Holy Spirit In You

Francis Chan, *The Forgotten God* (Colorado Springs, CO: David S. Cook, 2009) Chapter 1.

Andrew Murray, *Experiencing the Holy Spirit* (New Kensington, PA: Whitaker House, 2000)

Session 7: Crossing the Jordan

In the Mirror of God's Word (Cumming, GA: Jennifer Brommet, 2019)

About the Authors

This study was a collaborative effort by the following four authors. All have written additional *True Identity* materials and have taught at various True Identity retreats and conferences.

Jennifer Brommet hails from Wisconsin and has a background in photography and graphic design. She worked for the Billy Graham Evangelistic Association (BGEA) as Art Director in Minneapolis, Minnesota, and Production Coordinator for the 1986 BGEA International Conference for Itinerant Evangelists in Amsterdam, the Netherlands. While living in Amsterdam, she met and married her husband, Remco.

God prepared Jennifer for the call to start and lead *True Identity Ministries* through her own personal journey from severe rejection and depression as a child and young adult to freedom through understanding and embracing her TRUE Identity in Christ. She has a deep passion for others to understand how much God loves them, know His Word of truth, deepen their relationship with Him, and be set free to be all He designed and desires for them to be.

Jennifer has over thirty years of experience in ministry which has included; organizing and leading retreats and events, as well as teaching and speaking nationally and internationally, leading Bible study groups and small groups, marriage ministry with her husband, and serving as the Women's Ministry Director at her church in California, before moving to Georgia in 2007 and founding *True Identity Ministries* in 2008.

Jennifer began taking photos with a Brownie camera when she was eight years old and has spent a lifetime capturing God's beautiful creation through a camera lens. She also enjoys expressing herself creatively through drawing, sewing, decorating and design. She loves to travel, see new places and meet new people, and one of her favorite things is "writing with God."

Jennifer is a blended personality of Peaceful/Purposeful with spiritual gifts of exhortation, teaching and pastoring. She and Remco live in the north Atlanta, Georgia area while their two grown daughters pursue their dreams.

Judy Mills is a life-long Southerner now living in the heart of New York City with her husband Nelson. She's a friend of True Identity Ministries with the God-given personality of a Playful , and spiritual gifts in teaching, pastoring and hospitality.

Judy served in Community Bible Study for 12 years as a core leader, Children's Director and Teaching Director. She has written and taught numerous Bible studies, including *The Ultimate Joy: A Journey in Intimacy with God.* She currently serves as a women's ministry leader at Church of the City NYC, where she teaches and mentors young women. Additionally, she leads with Pray.NYC, a movement of prayer for spiritual awakening in New York City.

She has three adult children, one daughter-in-law, three (adorable!) granddaughters and is mother-in-law to two young men.

Photo by Emily Fletke Photography   *www.emilyfletkephotography.com*

Debbie Jones might tell you *"the East Coast"* when asked where she comes from because she has lived in seven east coast states, some twice! She attended the University of Florida and graduated with a BA in Anthropology.

After graduation Debbie worked in Social Services, but when her son was young, she began serving in children's ministry at church and later in preschool. Her love for the Bible and Bible study has prompted her to serve in Community Bible Study as a children's teacher and as a small group leader.

However the passion of her heart is inner healing prayer ministry. First trained as a prayer minister in 1998, she continues to receive training and pray with those in need of inner healing.

Debbie and her husband David, an entrepreneur, enjoy country living outside of Athens GA. They have a son, daughter-in-law and grandchildren in Atlanta.

Her first encounter with True Identity Ministries was attending the second women's retreat in spring 2009. She has remained an active participant and team member since then. In her words, *"I saw God working in True Identity and I wanted to join Him!"*

Remco Brommet was born and raised in the Netherlands, where he met Jennifer in 1985. After getting married in 1986, he moved with Jennifer to the US. He is somewhat of a globe trotter – he came to Christ at age 18 while living in Singapore. He earned a diploma in Missions Studies from Moorlands Bible College in Great Britain, and led movements of prayer for revival and spiritual awakening in the Upper Midwest and Southern California in the US before moving to the Atlanta area in 2007. His ministry experience also includes pastorates and jail, law enforcement and fire chaplaincies.

After receiving direction from the Lord that the *True Identity* message was to impact every populated continent of the world and seeing doors open in East Africa and Latin America, Remco took on the role of International Ministries Director. He is also an integral part of our materials development team adapting the material for men, and co-writing the *True Marriage* program and *TRUEPersonality* profile with Jennifer.

Remco holds dual citizenship in the US and The Netherlands. In addition to being a pastor, chaplain, speaker, prayer mobilizer and writer, he is an intercessor for spiritual awakening, revival and global missions. Above all he is a Christ-follower, devoted husband to Jennifer and father to adult daughters, Carina and Sophia.

About True Identity Ministries

⑪ TRUEIDENTITY
M I N I S T R I E S

True Identity Ministries, Inc. is a 501(c)3 non-profit, non-denominational ministry passionate about helping people come to know fully who and whose they are in Christ - helping them to know God's Word of TRUTH and to walk freely in all He designed and purposed for them to be.

True Identity Ministries was founded in 2008 by Jennifer Brommet in the Atlanta, Georgia area. What began as a retreat ministry to women has expanded to a transformational ministry for men and women around the globe! The *True Identity* teaching and materials have developed over the years to now include Online studies, videos, and resources. *TRUE Marriage*, a program to help couples understand God's design for marriage and discover the mission God has for *their* marriage, started in August of 2016 by Remco & Jennifer Brommet.

The *True Identity Message* has been shared with thousands in the U.S., East Africa, and Latin America and we praise God for the transformational work HE has done in setting His sons and daughters free in their true identity!

MORE INFO & CONTACT:
True Identity Ministries, Inc.
Email: info@TrueIdentityMinistries.org
Website: www.TrueIdentityMinistries.org
True Identity Studies website: www.TrueIdentityStudy.com

True Identity Ministries depends on the generous gifts of individuals and churches to help us continue to take the *True Identity Message* and resources around the globe. DONATE ONLINE on our website and help others be set free in their True Identity! All donations are tax deductible.

We also greatly appreciate your prayers! Check out our website for more information on how you an become a member of our Prayer Team. Thank you!

Jennifer's dramatic story of severe rejection and depression due to a birth defect is woven in with the *True Identity Message*. It is written in a way it can be used as a small group or personal study. Includes chapter questions, photos and resource diagrams. Chapters of the book are also tied in to and referenced in the *True Identity Study Guide*.

You can purchase the book or e Book through the *True Identity* website. It is also available on Amazon.

All proceeds from the book go to *True Identity Ministries* to help spread the *True Identity Message* around the globe!

TRUE IDENTITY STUDY SERIES

TrueIdentityStudy.com

True Identity Study #1
TRUE IDENTITY

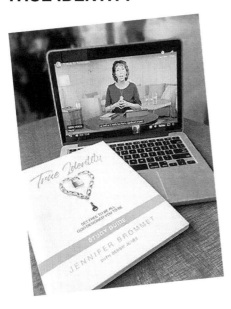

10 Session Study including:

- Easy to follow Study Guide
- Follow-along Session teaching videos
- Core Principles, Reflection Questions
- Group Discussion Questions, activities and prayer
- Personal stories
- Additional resources

Sessions include:

- Personality - including TRUEPersonality assessment
- Mistaken Identity
- Lies
- Breaking the Chains
- True Identity
- Walking in Your True Identity

True Identity Study #2
WALKING IN YOUR TRUE IDENTITY

7 Session Study including:

- Easy to follow Study Guide
- Helps in implementing what was learned in the first *True Identity Study* and how to deepen your relationship and walk with God
- Self-Study format and learning helps & tools
- Self-study Guide, Core Principles, Reflection Questions
- Group Discussion Questions, activity and prayer
- Brief videos from the session author with a session overview and personal example
- Additional resources

Sessions include:

- Saved From and Saved For
- Intimacy with God & Hearing from God
- The Holy Spirit in You & Spiritual Gifts
- Crossing the Jordan & Walk On!